ASSET PROTECTION PLANNING FOR SENIORS

ASSET PROTECTION PLANNING FOR SENIORS

Michael A. Babiarz, J.D.

iUniverse, Inc.
New York Lincoln Shanghai

ASSET PROTECTION PLANNING FOR SENIORS

iUniverse books may be ordered through booksellers or by contacting:

iUniverse
2021 Pine Lake Road, Suite 100
Lincoln, NE 68512
www.iuniverse.com
1-800-Authors (1-800-288-4677)

Because of the dynamic nature of the Internet, any Web addresses or links contained in this book may have changed since publication and may no longer be valid.

The information, ideas, and suggestions in this book are not intended to render legal advice. Before following any suggestions contained in this book, you should consult your personal attorney. Neither the author nor the publisher shall be liable or responsible for any loss or damage allegedly arising as a consequence of your use or application of any information or suggestions in this book.

ISBN: 978-0-595-45777-9 (pbk)
ISBN: 978-0-595-69675-8 (cloth)
ISBN: 978-0-595-90079-4 (ebk)

Printed in the United States of America

First Edition 1998
Laura M. Bertram, Editor

Second Edition 2004

Third Edition 2007
Ann M. Babiarz, Editor

Contents

1

What is This Book About, Anyway?

What <u>is</u> this book about, anyway? Who should be reading this book? Exactly how do we hope to impart some small bits of wit and wisdom upon you, the unsuspecting reader?

This book will cover, in a breezy, conversational style, the three biggest issues that face seniors and their families today. All these concerns relate to protecting the nest egg that you may have accumulated through a life of hard work, careful planning, and sometimes, a little luck as well.

The first concern is how to protect your nest egg if you become incompetent. If that happens, who will pay your bills? File your tax returns? Protect your assets from abuse by those who might prey upon an infirm elder? Many times, a person plans carefully for her retirement years. Investment strategies, tax planning, even estate planning can be put into motion. How can you ensure that any careful plans you have set forth will stay in motion and not stall because of some unforeseen illness? Often, the lack of capacity or competency is brought on slowly by the most horrific of maladies, such as Alzheimer's disease or other forms of dementia. Other times competency is lost suddenly from stroke or other trauma.

The illnesses or accidents that cause a lack of competency often foreshadow the most final of asset protection threats: death. What happens if you should pass away? Will the plans you have laid to take care of your spouse and family remain intact? Will your estate be settled in the court system? Will Uncle Sam's taxman be waiting with arms outstretched to collect his fair share (or more) of your estate? What if you have a "problem child" in the family who will pop up if you die, causing misery to the other family members who truly cared for you during your life? What if you remarried? Will your children from a first marriage be remembered? What if your children, good souls though they may be, have miseries of their own that would imperil receipt of an inheritance from you, such as creditors upon their doorstep, or ex-spouses? Our second set of issues focuses upon the continuing protection of your nest egg for your spouse and family even in the event of your death.

Finally, the nest egg may not even make it to that point if it is depleted by the cost of long-term care. Perhaps the most devastating threat to your assets is the very real chance that you or your spouse may spend significant time in your later years in a nursing home. At a monthly cost of $4,500 to $6,000 or more, even a substantial nest egg can be reduced to nothing in a very short time. Planning to help your nest egg survive the "residence of last resort" is a key to asset protection planning for your later years.

This is a terrible trio of grim sounding problems. What we hope to do over the course of this book is to address these concerns in as light a style as possible. Sometimes, our examples have a little fun with the problems of life. We don't mean to belittle the problems. We sure don't want to offend anyone. However, sometimes facing the reality of these issues with a positive attitude helps in formulating the best of plans. What will this book NOT do? This is not a "form book" or a "do it yourself" guide. We firmly believe that those texts are at best irresponsible and at worst dangerous. What this book will do is help you to ask the right questions. It may not necessarily provide you with all the answers to your questions. Knowing the right questions to ask is more important in the long run. There is no way that a formbook or guide can provide a solution to everyone's situation. Even the best of these types of texts invariably try to force fit your circumstances into a pre-set solution. In asset protection planning, there is no "one size fits all" arrangement. Every plan must be tailored to a specific set of facts.

This book is also not a technical manual. You will not find overly technical language or extensive charts, figures or lengthy texts on minute details. Purists among you may note that some concerns are simplified for clarity. Writers among you may shudder at the informal style we use. The book extensively uses examples to show how a concern can arise and some right and wrong ways it can be addressed. As you peruse each chapter in this book, building upon the knowledge you gain, you will slowly see how your plan can be formulated.

Each chapter in this book builds upon the knowledge that you gain from the previous ones. Each chapter is designed to cause you to think about your personal situation. As you go through the text, hopefully, you will take stock of your affairs. Reading with a highlighter in hand or a pen and paper by your side is definitely recommended!

Chapters 2 through 5 deal with our first issue: incompetence. Chapter 2 defines incompetency and the types of problems it causes. Chapter 3 outlines the most popular approach to the problem of incompetency: not doing anything until the problem arises. Chapter 4 talks about some informal kinds of things people often do when thinking about the difficulties of incompetency. Chapter 5 looks to some more formal tools, such as powers of attorney and trusts aimed at helping you to take a proactive approach to combat incompetency before it arises.

Our next set of chapters examines how death impacts the asset protection process. Chapter 6 focuses on probate—the court proceeding that settles some estates—and when it will and will not be needed to settle your estate. Chapter 7 revisits trusts, looking at the trust not only as an incompetency protection tool, but also as a plan to settle your estate when you die. Chapter 8 compares the use of trusts with wills and other types of tools designed to pass assets at death. Our ninth chapter attempts to describe, in as simple terms as possible, how the federal government taxes your estate when you die. Finally, Chapter 10 spotlights the problems of beneficiaries to your estate. This chapter looks at how you can protect your estate from being depleted by estate contests, attachment by creditors or ex-spouses of beneficiaries, or other perils.

The final section of the book builds upon what we have learned about incompetency and death. These chapters deal with the issue of long-term care and how it can deplete your estate. Chapter 11 delves into the residence of last resort—the nursing home—and how and when the decision is made for you or a family member to reside there. Chapter 12 covers the basic rules of the Medicaid system, which is the government's only real program to assist you in paying for long-term care. Chapters 13 and 14 review how the Medicaid rules allow for you to create certain types of asset protection plans to shelter your assets. Finally, Chapter 15 ties in some of the content addressed in the previous set of chapters when we discover how to protect inheritances for the family if Medicaid is paying the bills for care in a nursing home.

Our last chapter is Chapter 16. Chapter 16 shows how all these issues can be addressed in a comprehensive plan. In this chapter, we will follow three hypothetical family situations. Each situation will present us with some challenges that we can solve using the knowledge gained from the previous chapters in the book. Again, while these fictional families may not be exactly the same as yours—because no two families are alike—you will see how a plan can be put together. Remember that you will need to tailor your plan to your exact situation.

Asset Protection Planning for Seniors is aimed primarily at the senior citizen and her (or his) children. Often, older adults rely upon their children to help them understand some of the issues they face. Many seniors, though, remain fiercely independent throughout the "golden years." This book will speak directly to you as well!

2

Who's Minding the Store? Incompetency and the Problems It Causes

Statistics show that approximately eight of every ten Americans will at some point in their lives be incompetent. Incompetency, in the sense that it impacts upon the estate planning and asset protection process, can be defined as the inability, due to illness, mental or physical deterioration, or accident, to make or communicate decisions regarding your personal or financial affairs or both. This inability can be either due to mental factors such as Alzheimer's disease or dementia or physical factors such as unconsciousness or coma.

About eight of ten Americans now die in a hospital, and roughly seven of every ten persons will either have to make a decision about a close family member, or have a decision made about themselves, regarding the termination of life-sustaining medical treatment at the end of life. With longer life spans comes the greater probability that age related concerns such as dementia, or other illnesses or maladies, will cause incompetency in a member of your household.

If you become incompetent, two questions arise: Who can make a health-care decision on your behalf if you are unable? *And* who can handle your financial affairs if you cannot? These twin problems are the focus of this chapter as well as Chapters 3, 4 and 5.

Healthcare decision-making ability is the first issue raised when someone becomes incompetent. It is also the most important, as potentially, someone can have the power to alter where you live, how you live, and even if you live. We can divide healthcare decisions into two major groups: those that involve routine issues and those that involve life-sustaining issues.

Initially, whether dealing with either routine or life-sustaining healthcare decisions, we must start with a simple premise. You are competent to make your own healthcare decisions, routine to life sustaining, until and unless it is determined you cannot do so. You have the right to consent to or refuse any medical care. No one can force care upon you that you do not wish. Stories abound in newspapers and on television of people who, for religious, personal, or other reasons, refuse certain kinds of medical care. You have a fundamental right, guaranteed by the U.S. Constitution, as well as the constitutions of most states, to be secure in the integrity of your body. This right extends to the right to make decisions about your healthcare.

With this right so strongly rooted, the law presumes competency. Determining lack of competency can be a difficult conclusion to reach. For the moment, however, let us assume that either you or your spouse is incompetent. Routine as well as life sustaining care may be at issue.

What specific types of concerns are we discussing when we discuss these healthcare decisions?

EXAMPLE:

George and Gracie, now in their 80s, have been happily married for over 50 years. They have two children, Ronnie and Sandy, to whom they are very close. Gracie has been diagnosed with middle stages of probable Alzheimer's disease. She also suffers from a mild form of depression. Her physician, Dr. Von Zell, feels Gracie is not competent to make any healthcare decisions. Gracie has not done any planning to prepare for this situation. George and his children reluctantly believe that Gracie should be admitted to a nursing home. George simply cannot care for her any longer at home. Gracie will also be safer in the nursing home. While in the family home, Gracie has been wandering out the door and down the street, getting lost, and crossing busy streets without looking. In general, Gracie is endangering herself. She is also refusing to eat. Dr. Von Zell believes that Gracie would benefit from medication to alleviate some of the symptoms of her depression. Unfortunately, Gracie does not want to enter a nursing home, and she is refusing to take medication. George wants to sign her into the nursing home. He also wants to force Gracie to eat. Ronnie wants to get a second opinion from another doctor about the diagnosis of depression and wants copies of Gracie's medical records from Dr. Von Zell. Sandy feels that the diagnosis of depression is correct and wants her mother to begin drug therapy immediately. With Gracie seemingly unable to do so herself, who has the legal right to determine where she lives, to force her to eat, to decide what medicines she might receive, and to examine what is contained in her medical records: George? Ronnie? Sandy?

Surprisingly, the correct legal answer to this question is none of the above! Without any legal authority to speak on behalf of Gracie, even George, her spouse of 50 years, is not Gracie's guardian, surrogate or legal caregiver of any kind. In situations like George and Gracie, however, many medical providers will honor the "informal" approach that has been in place for centuries. They will turn to next of kin for these decisions. In our example, Dr. Van Zell might conduct a family conference with George, Ronnie and Sandy to reach a consensus. Increasingly, doctors and healthcare facilities are becoming concerned about the liability of dealing with family members informally. They are insisting on more clear lines of legal authority to act on behalf of an unquestionably incompetent person.

In addition to the routine medical decisions posed by George and Gracie, the question of withholding or withdrawing life-sustaining care is often in the press. George also wonders about Gracie's refusal to eat. Suppose she receives drug therapy for her depression yet still refuses food. Is this a "life-sustaining care" issue? For every Dr. Kevorkian accused of assisting in suicide, there are thousands of terminally ill patients and their families wondering whether respirators, feeding tubes, or other care is appropriate. Could Gracie be force-fed? Or, what if she were comatose? Who would decide whether life saving equipment should be imposed?

EXAMPLE:

> George Clark, age 84, suffers from a form of dementia. His illness has progressed to the point where he no longer recognizes anyone even Lois, his wife of 60 years, or his children, Jimmy and Alice. On top of this, George had a stroke and is now comatose. His physician, Dr. Leslie, has told Lois and the children George has suffered severe brain damage. Even if he were to recover from the coma, his functioning level would be extremely low. A ventilator is assisting George's breathing. Dr. Leslie now tells Lois and the children that without a feeding tube, George will likely die soon. Lois and the children do not want the feeding tube inserted. Moreover, they would prefer that the ventilator be discontinued as well. George has almost no hope of any recovery from his current condition, and the family believes that he would not wish to be kept alive in this manner. George never planned in advance for this situation. He has no written documents that express how he might feel about life support. Can the family refuse the feeding tube? Can they request that the ventilator be withdrawn?

The first widely reported instances of the "right to die" as it is commonly known, appeared in the mid 1970s. A debate soon ensued as to what rights a person has, if any, to refuse life sustaining care when he or she is unable to make the decision. Medical science and the healing arts progressed to a point where the body could be kept alive long after the person's higher brain functions have departed.

The current state of the law is more settled than 30 years ago. You now have the right in every state to place instructions refusing life-sustaining care into various widely accepted documents. Further, in some states, statutes exist that give family members or a court-appointed guardian the right to make these decisions on your behalf if you have not prepared any documents in advance. In states where no statute exists, courts have decided that family can exercise the right to refuse life-sustaining care on behalf of a hopelessly ill patient. While the law may have made more provisions for these situations, two glaring gaps still appear.

One gap in the law is knowing what the person would want if he had not put it on paper. In our example above, does Lois, Jimmy or Alice know for sure what George would want in that situation? As his spouse of 60 years, Lois may have some assurance that she knows George's feelings. But what if Lois were deceased, and Jimmy or Alice had to decide? What if Jimmy and Alice had lived out of state for the last 30 years and were no longer close to George?

The other gap, if it may be called that, is a more controversial one. The law places considerable distinction among passively refusing treatment, removing treatment, and assisting in suicide. Every state recognizes the right to refuse treatment. Most allow someone to request that treatment currently in place be removed, viewing it as a right to refuse continued treatment. Assisting in suicide—the active role in causing death—is considered taboo in the U.S. Assisted suicide is accepted in some other areas of the world, such as the Netherlands.

EXAMPLE:

> Let's continue with our example. Lois, Jimmy and Alice meet with Dr. Leslie to discuss George's condition. Dr. Leslie has no problem honoring the family's request that the feeding tube not be implanted. Dr. Leslie is a little uncomfortable about withdrawing the ventilator. Dr. Leslie also reacts negatively to Jimmy's suggestion that his father could receive extra dosages of morphine to end his suffering. The "shot of morphine" is viewed by the doctor as assisted suicide, and forbidden under the laws where George lives. Dr. Leslie is a little uncomfortable removing a ventilator, as that affirmative act will probably allow George to die. However, the laws where George lives will probably permit this. The most acceptable act in this situation is the refusal of additional treatment: the feeding tube.

A further complication might have arisen if the family wanted to remove a feeding tube already in place. Removal of water and food, which may cause death by dehydration or starvation, often sparks another round of debate. Is the provision of food and water "medical care" that is being withdrawn?

Finally, a new wrinkle to the healthcare decision making conundrum was added in 2003. Amendments to a federal healthcare law, known by its acronym HIPAA, now prohibit the release of private medical information to anyone not authorized to receive it. Family members and even spouses are not automatically allowed to obtain medical information about an incompetent family member without written consent of some type. Lacking information, it is difficult if not impossible to monitor and advocate for the healthcare needs of an ill family member.

The second problem that arises when a person loses competency is a non-medical one: the ability to make financial decisions. If you lose capacity to make healthcare decisions, you usually do not have the ability to manage your finances either. Who then steps in to make sure bills are paid, assets safeguarded, and tax returns filed? The lack of ability to manage finances is our second issue that arises where competency is lost.

EXAMPLE:

> Mickey, age 74, and his wife Ruthie, age 72, run a small manufacturing business that employs 10 people. Mickey suffers a stroke and his physician, Dr. Bing, tells Ruthie that Mickey is no longer competent to manage his affairs. Ruthie wonders how Mickey's business will be run. She wants to sell shares of stock that Mickey owns in Entertainment, Inc. to pay medical bills. She and Mickey own the stock jointly. Finally, their accountant has finished the income tax return for the year. He needs both of their signatures on the return.

The lack of ability to manage financial affairs can be a wide-ranging problem. Someone who lacks capacity may not be able to: (1) run a business; (2) write a check; (3) endorse and cash or deposit a check; (4) sign a tax return; (5) access assets held in his own name or held with others jointly; (6) sell, lease or otherwise deal with real estate; (7) make a withdrawal from an IRA or company retirement plan; (8) get into a safe deposit box; (9) prepare a new will; (10) change a beneficiary on a life insurance policy; or (11) sue or defend himself in a lawsuit. This list is not all-inclusive. If you think of all the ways you manage your personal and business financial life, you will find that every single day you make some sort of financial decision. Most of us do not plan for someone to step into our shoes if we become ill or disabled in some way.

Like healthcare decision-making, the same presumption of competency exists with financial management. You are presumed competent until determined to be otherwise. The loss of ability to manage your finances or healthcare does not occur simply because of age or illness. It is rarely a physical problem.

When does a person become incompetent? Incompetency can sometimes occur in a single defining event, like a stroke or an auto accident. More often, it results from a gradual loss of cognitive functioning, due to dementia, Alzheimer's disease, or other chronic illness.

Competency is not like a light bulb controlled by an on-off switch. It is more like a light bulb operated by a dimmer switch. As you turn the dimmer switch the light bulb becomes dimmer. At some point the light bulb becomes too dim to do its job. Similarly, a person's mental abilities usually fail gradually, until at some point he or she is no longer able to manage their affairs. Often, persons have limited capacity, meaning they have the ability to make some, but not all healthcare or financial decisions.

Competency is a slippery slope. Sometimes determining incompetency is easy. For example, a comatose person can be safely deemed to be incompetent. What about a person with mid-stage dementia? When is he incompetent?

Medical professionals such as doctors, social workers and nurses have several tools they use to measure capacity. Often, these are tests that evaluate long and short term memory, as well as how oriented someone is as to person, place, and time. You are oriented as to person if you know who you are, and who your family and close friends are. You are oriented as to place if you know where you are; you can be oriented to time if you know general times of day. For example, you ate lunch so the next meal is dinner; you do not awake at 3 AM and get dressed for breakfast, etc.

So when are you deemed incompetent? There is a legal answer to this question. There is a practical answer as well.

You are legally incompetent when either a court declares you to be so, or a statute permits a medical provider to so determine. For example, many states have statutes that allow family members to make life sustaining healthcare decisions on behalf of incompetent persons. Typically, a physician must make an initial determination under these statutes that the person is not capable of making decisions. Then the family can step in. This determination may be limited to only life sustaining care issues, however, and may not pertain to routine medical care or financial matters. The lack of capacity to make routine health care decisions or to manage one's finances can be legally determined by a court in a guardianship proceeding. (We will discuss guardianship in our next two chapters.) When the court makes this determination in a court order, or a doctor so states under the rules set forth in a statute as to certain types of medical care, you will be declared legally incompetent.

Legal incompetency is easily defined. Practical incompetency is trickier. The practical answer often occurs when someone either challenges your actions or refuses to engage with you in a business transaction.

EXAMPLE:

Jackie has lived alone since the loss of his wife, Audrey. He has two children, a son, Art, and a daughter, Jane. Art lives next door, but Jane lives out of state. Jackie is suffering from dementia and is extremely disorientated. He no longer remembers where he lives, and thinks the year is 1955. He thinks Audrey is at the store and wonders when she will return. He arises at 3:00 AM, dressing himself in his old bus driver's uniform to go to work, even though he retired many years ago. Jackie lived quite frugally and amassed a sizeable estate by selling kitchen utensils on television. Art takes Jackie to the neighborhood law offices, the Brooklyn Legal Clinic. He wants Jackie to make a will that leaves Jackie's entire estate to him. The attorney at the Clinic refuses to prepare the will, believing Jackie is not competent to make one. Art, not to be deterred, takes Jackie to another firm, Dewey, Cheatum, and Howe. Attorney Dewey prepares the will. Art then has Jackie transfer most of his assets to him. He then admits Jackie to Gotham Nursing Home. Art has Jackie sign an application for Medicaid to pay for the nursing home. He deliberately states on the application that Jackie has no assets nor has Jackie given any assets away. Jackie dies shortly thereafter. Jane comes into town and finds what Art has done. She wants to challenge the will and all the transfers. She understands that the Brooklyn Legal Clinic refused to prepare the will but that Attorney Dewey drafted one anyway.

Practically speaking, was Jackie incompetent when he made the will? When he allowed Art to transfer all the assets to himself? When he signed the application for Medicaid? Can Jane contest these actions? Most important, what could Jackie have done earlier to protect himself from this abuse? What could Jane have done after Jackie became too confused to plan, but prior to Art committing any of his nefarious acts?

Competency, and its lack, leads to questions about financial acts, as well as healthcare decisions. Who can step in to make sure that you are adequately cared for and that you are not financially abused? Statistically, less than 10% of all Americans have any kind of plan in place to protect themselves from the ills created by a loss of competency. Planning in advance is the best alternative. If it is too late for that to occur, protection for the incompetent can be had too. Because of the enormous cost of healthcare and the potential for financial mismanagement or abuse, incompetency poses a serious threat to the protection of your assets. Our next chapters look at both planning in advance of incompetency and measures to take if competency is already lost.

3

The "No Plan" Approach: Guardianships, Conservatorships and Their Brethren

In our last chapter, we looked at the twin problems that lack of competency causes. A person who lacks competency may need assistance in managing his or her finances and in making personal and healthcare decisions. Planning in advance to avoid the need for a court to become involved is the preferable alternative. We will look at some informal as well as formal plans in Chapters 4 and 5. If you have not made any plans and you lose capacity, what happens then?

<u>EXAMPLE:</u>

> Desi and Lucy are husband and wife of many years. Desi suffered a stroke and no longer recognizes his family. He thinks the year is 1959 and believes that his apartment is a nightclub. Desi has several bank accounts that are in his name alone. He also owns one-half of a small business, together with his partner, Ricky. Desi has an aversion to lawyers, and has no documents of any kind to designate anyone to make personal or financial decisions for him. Lucy needs to get access to Desi's bank accounts to pay bills, but finds that the bank refuses to let her draw money from his account. Ricky has received an offer to sell the business, and feels it might be a very good deal for all concerned. Desi's doctor thinks that Desi should be placed in Hollywood Hills Nursing Home. Lucy goes to court to become Desi's guardian. As guardian she can access his accounts, deal with business affairs, and consult with his doctors.

If no plans are made, and you lose capacity, establishing a guardianship may be the only answer. Guardianship is typically viewed as a last resort, where other means are not available. Guardianships are used when someone loses capacity to make personal and financial decisions. It is a court proceeding. Even if your spouse wants to be your guardian, he or she must petition the court to be appointed.

There are several kinds of guardianships, each appropriate in different settings. Someone can be a temporary guardian, a plenary (or permanent and full) guardian, a guardian of the person only, a guardian of the estate, or conservator, only, or both guardian of the person and estate. Limited guardianships are also possible.

If you are not competent, and have a medical concern that requires immediate attention, a family member or other individual may ask the court, on very short notice, for permission to be your temporary guardian. The temporary guardian usually has powers that last only for a brief period, and only those powers that are specifically authorized by the court.

A more common guardianship is a plenary guardianship. Most often, if someone cannot make decisions, he or she is unable to manage both person and finances. Sometimes however, only a financial, or estate guardianship is needed, as a person may lack the ability to manage money, but still can make medical or similar personal decisions. A plenary guardian of the estate or conservatorship is the answer. If a person has little or no funds, a guardianship of the estate may not be necessary. In those cases, a plenary guardian of the person is appointed.

Many states now have provisions for limited guardianships. Because a guardianship is a proceeding of last resort, courts will look to the least restrictive alternative that still protects the individual. If a person lacks some, but not all ability to make decisions, a court could appoint a limited guardian of the person, of the estate or both.

EXAMPLE:

> Lucy learns from Desi's doctor that Desi is in immediate need of heart surgery. Lucy petitions the court to be temporary guardian of Desi's person so that she can make medical decisions for him. She also petitions to be plenary (permanent) guardian of his person and estate. The temporary petition is granted, within a few days, so that Desi's surgery can go forward without delay. Several weeks later, a brief court hearing occurs at which Lucy is appointed plenary guardian. Lucy can now access Desi's accounts, work with Ricky on a possible sale of the business, and move Desi from the rehab center where he went after his surgery to Hollywood Hills Nursing Home.

A guardianship of any type, if uncontested, is generally a perfunctory court proceeding. The starting point for any petition for guardianship is a medical report from a physician. A doctor's evaluation is necessary for a court to judge someone incompetent. The medical report must specifically state the reasons why the person cannot make decisions, and if he or she is totally or partially incapacitated. The medical report must be based on a recent evaluation of the person. Further, the medical report must show that a guardian is required. Eccentric or unpopular behavior by itself is not grounds for guardianship.

EXAMPLE:

> Henry Walden, age 78, lives in a small cabin in the woods outside of town. He is an ardent supporter of a fringe political party, and devotes much of his spare time writing articles and letters to the editor about his partisan preferences. His companions are two dogs and six cats. His children are dismayed over his behavior and visit the local attorney, Mr. Emerson, to see if one of them can be made guardian. Attorney Emerson tells them to have Henry evaluated by his doctor first. The doctor's report finds that while Henry may be an unusual man, he is well oriented, has no significant memory loss and is generally in good physical and mental health. Attorney Emerson advises the Walden children that they have no grounds to impose a guardianship upon their father. Had they had a medical report that showed he was incapacitated, further inquiry could be made.

Assuming that an adequate medical report is obtained, a petition is filed with the court and a hearing date set. Prior to the hearing, all close relatives receive a copy of the petition and notice of the court date by mail. The person for whom a guardian is sought must be served with a summons, like any other lawsuit. The summons affords an alleged incompetent person the opportunity to object to the guardianship.

At the hearing date, if the incompetent person does not come forward with objections, all the procedural safeguards are met, and the medical report is clear, the judge will appoint the guardian designated in the petition. Generally, a family member will ask to be appointed, although banks or trust companies sometimes act as guardians of the estate. In some states, state agencies exist to be guardians for those who have no family or family that do not wish to serve as guardian.

A guardianship may be contested. The person for whom the guardian is sought can object, and has the right to a more formal trial on the issue of his competency. Further, another family member or person can come forward to file a competing petition (usually called a cross petition) agreeing that a guardian is necessary, but disputing that the person seeking to be guardian in the first petition is a good choice. A trial is also necessary to decide between competing petitions.

EXAMPLE:

Henry Walden's son, Ralph, disregards Attorney Emerson's advice, and files for guardianship anyway. Mr. Walden's daughter files a cross petition. Henry himself retains a lawyer and files objections to any guardianship. A trial date is set for a hearing on all the petitions.

Contested guardianships can often be the most bitter fights in court this side of divorces. "Dirty laundry" is often aired as family members attempt to show why one or the other would be a poor guardian, or why a parent or other family member is incompetent. Trials in guardianship court are often expensive and messy affairs.

Assuming a guardian is ultimately appointed, what does she do? Once the court appoints a guardian, the matter is not concluded. The court retains jurisdiction over the guardianship for the life of the incompetent person. In other words, the case continues until death. The guardian must file an inventory of all the assets of the incompetent person's estate, and file accountings on an annual or other court required basis. Accountings detail all income and expenditures the guardian makes on behalf of the incompetent individual. A guardian, even if a spouse, must post a surety bond. The bond is a yearly cost that is based on the value of the assets in the guardianship estate. This bond would reimburse the incapacitated person if the guardian steals or mismanages the money. Courts may also require the guardian to get specific permission to move the individual, to spend money over set amounts, to consent to serious medical procedures, and the like. It is an intrusive, expensive, and time-consuming process.

The expense, time, and intrusiveness of a guardianship are good practical reasons why a guardianship is a procedure of last resort. From a legal standpoint, a guardianship removes rights from an individual. Sometimes, a person judged in court to be incompetent cannot vote, drive a car, get married, get divorced, choose where they live, choose their doctor, enter into contracts, or buy or sell property, even their own.

These restrictions are why courts treat guardianships seriously. Usually, a person seeking guardianship over another has to prove by convincing evidence that a guardian is needed. This high standard is necessary as the court tries to balance protection of an alleged incompetent individual with the need to respect individual rights.

The laws that allow appointment of a guardian give preference first to family members in an order corresponding roughly to the degree of kinship. A spouse typically has the highest priority, followed by children. If a person has no spouse or children, or none that wish to act, courts next look to other relatives such as brothers or sisters, grandchildren, or others. If no family members are available or willing to act, state or county agencies exist to step in. Some private guardianship services exist that will act as private guardians for individuals who have no family or whose family does not choose to act.

Another option for an estate guardianship is a bank or trust company. Banks can be a good choice, particularly if the incompetent individual has extensive holdings, runs one or more businesses, or if well-meaning family members who would be guardian lack financial sophistication themselves. Having a bank serve as estate guardian may eliminate the need for a surety bond, saving the estate considerable expense. A bank or trust company cannot act as a personal guardian in most states, however. Thus, if a bank is to act as estate guardian, and the person also needs a personal guardian, then an appropriate individual must be sought.

The order of preference of a guardian can be altered if a person has nominated a specific individual to be a guardian if one is necessary. In most states, a document signed by you, and witnessed by one or two witnesses, affords you the opportunity to pick someone of your choice as guardian. For example, if you have no spouse, but have three children, and trust one child over the other two, you may designate that child as your guardian if one is needed. A nomination of guardian does not make that child guardian absent a court hearing. The court can also override your choice if it finds that the person you selected is not appropriate. The court will give great weight to your preference, and without evidence showing that your choice is flawed, will honor your request.

Many state laws also set forth requirements for a guardian. A guardian must always be an adult, usually defined by state law as either age 18 or 21. Sometimes, the law states that a guardian must reside in the state where the incompetent person lives. Often, state laws prohibit persons from serving as guardian if they have criminal records or a history of mental instability.

A guardian is under the scrutiny and supervision of the courts. The courts will be involved in significant financial and personal decisions that the guardian will make on behalf of his ward. Acting as guardian can be a time consuming job. Further, a guardian must keep good records. Courts will allow a guardian to be compensated from the funds of the incompetent person. For individual guardians, compensation is limited to a modest hourly rate, and allowed only if the incompetent person has sufficient funds to pay the fees without jeopardizing his own needs.

If the guardian dies, becomes ill, or for good reason wants to terminate his responsibilities as guardian, the court will look to a petition for appointment of a successor guardian. The first guardian, or if he is ill or dead, someone acting on his behalf, must file a final accounting showing all assets turned over to the successor guardian. If a person judged incompetent regains competency, he can petition the court to have his rights restored and the guardianship terminated. Restoration hearings, as they are known, are rare. Occasionally, through therapy, hard work, or even a miracle someone becomes well again. A guardianship need not be forever if it is no longer needed.

Usually, however, a personal guardianship continues until the death of the ward. An estate guardianship can be closed prior to death if the incompetent person's funds are exhausted. If someone is to act as your guardian, or if you are asked to become a guardian for a family member, be aware that this is a long-term commitment. The guardianship court becomes a permanent part of the incompetent person's life and the guardian's life.

Given the intrusiveness of guardianships, and the aversion most people have to the court system, you may ask how a guardianship can be avoided. Plans, both informal and formal exist to obviate the need for appointment of a guardian. Chapter 4 looks at some informal plans that people make to provide for family to step in and assist if they become ill. Chapter 5 will look at more formal planning approaches. Both chapters discuss pros and cons of various approaches. Absent personal or financial abuse, a guardianship is generally something you should plan to avoid. Court intervention should be sought in cases of abuse. Fortunately, most of us have people we feel we can trust to help us in time of need. Our next two chapters will look at how we ensure that these trusted individuals can come to our aid.

4

Informal Planning:
Avoidance of the Lawyer's Office

The way in which you hold title to an asset affects the ability to control or deal with the asset during your life. By "asset," we mean anything you might own. Your house, bank accounts, stocks, bonds, and all other property can be titled in various ways. In addition to how you control an asset during your life, titling also affects the ultimate disposition of the asset upon death. Too often, persons engage in "informal" estate planning, using various forms of holding title, without fully understanding the consequences of their actions.

EXAMPLE:

> Marley Jones, an elderly widower, has four children. His son Max lives nearest him, and helps Mr. Jones manage his day-to-day affairs. Because Mr. Jones wants Max to pay Mr. Jones' bills if he became sick or injured, he changes title to all his bank accounts to "Marley Jones and Max Jones as joint tenants with rights of survivorship."

A joint tenancy like the one described above, is one form of holding title that you may already use. It is a type of informal estate planning. You may also have used various forms of beneficiary designations, such as "payable on death" on bank accounts. Holding title to property jointly with your spouse can be a good plan under many circumstances. Perils arise when someone other than a spouse is named as joint tenant.

With a joint tenancy, all persons own an equal interest in the property. Joint tenancy conveys to each "tenant" an equal and undivided interest in the property. Upon the death of one of the joint tenants, the surviving tenant or tenants become the sole owner(s) of the entire property by operation of law. The deceased joint tenant's will has no effect on the disposition of this property. In fact, property owed in joint tenancy will pass automatically to the surviving joint tenants even if the deceased's will contains contrary instructions.

EXAMPLE:

> Marley Jones dies after he placed his son Max on title as a joint tenant on all his bank accounts, totaling $200,000. Marley has a will that states that his four children are to receive his estate equally. Does Max have to abide by this will? No! Do the bank accounts belong to Max now because of the joint tenancies? Yes!

Another reason people create joint tenancies is that a joint tenancy will avoid "probate." Probate is a court proceeding; it will be discussed in detail in Chapter 6. Avoidance of probate when one spouse dies by titling property jointly between spouses is common in estate planning. But while it is true that probate is avoided upon the death of the first joint tenant, once the last joint tenant dies, all the property becomes subject to probate. And if both spouses perish in a common accident, joint tenancy may not be helpful, as probate may be needed for the estate of the second spouse to die. If the order of death cannot be proved, two probate estates, one for the husband and one for the wife, may be needed. Further, even if a spouse survives, and then tries to avoid probate at a later date by creating a joint tenancy with a non-spouse (e.g., a child), a host of other problems arise. We have already seen in our example that creation of a joint tenancy with only one of many children can result in the unintentional disinheritance of the other children. Children can also be left with no inheritance if the surviving spouse remarries, and creates new joint tenancies with the new spouse.

Another possible disadvantage of a joint tenancy with someone other than your spouse is the risks to which you now expose your property.

EXAMPLE:

> Jackie, a widower, has three children: Audrey, Art, and Sheila. Jackie's estate consists of some stocks, mutual funds, and his condo. He places the condo in a four-way joint tenancy with all three children. He re-titles his stocks and bank accounts into joint tenancies: some with Art, some with Audrey, and others with Sheila. Troubles arise down the road. Art announces that he is getting divorced. His attorney, June Taylor, is concerned that Art's soon-to-be ex-wife will try to lay claim to some of the assets Art holds jointly with Jackie. Sheila is the spend-thrift of the family, and her ways have finally done her in. She has $45,000 in credit card debt and no means to pay. Her creditors have already filed suit against her. She is considering bankruptcy. Not to be outdone, Audrey proves that Jackie has a truly dysfunctional family. Audrey is a lawyer who never bothered to obtain malpractice insur-ance. She botched a case that a bus company retained her to try. Now the bus company is suing her for malpractice and asking for $500,000 in damages. Are Jackie's assets safe in Art's divorce? From Sheila's cred-itors or possible bankruptcy? How about from Audrey's malfeasance? Unfortunately, the answers to each of these three questions may depend upon what a judge says!

When people are asked why they "put a child's name" on an account, con-venience is the most common reason given. "I want my child to be able to pay my bills if I am sick. I don't want my family's inheritance tied up in probate court."

It is true that bank accounts are easily accessible by a joint tenant. A trusted son or daughter can withdraw money from accounts to pay bills. A son or daughter who should not have been trusted can also drain the entire account without your consent! Utmost care needs to be taken when creat-ing a joint tenancy on a bank account because the law generally does not require a joint tenant to keep records or account for funds withdrawn.

If you become ill or disabled, some joint tenancies will not help. Creation of these joint tenancies instead become much more inconvenient than convenient. Many types of jointly held assets need the consent of <u>all</u> the joint tenants to be accessed, sold, or otherwise dealt with. Bank accounts can usually be accessed by either joint tenant, but these are an exception. Putting children on title to a house does not allow a child to deal with the house if you are sick. It merely increases the number of persons who must be competent to sign documents.

EXAMPLE:

> We revisit our friend Jackie. Jackie learns to his relief that his condo was only put into joint tenancy with Art and that Art's ex-wife is not making any claim to the condo. Jackie's sense of ease is short lived. The strain of the divorce caused Art to have a stroke. He is now comatose. Jackie would like to sell his condo, but finds that he needs Art's signature on the property deed. What should Jackie do? Perhaps he may consider seeking court appointment as Art's guardian.

Joint tenancy may also create undesirable tax consequences. Upon the death of one joint tenant, only one-half of the property receives the new "stepped up" tax basis, which is a new date of death value. Therefore, if the joint tenant sells the property, there may be unwanted capital gain consequences.

EXAMPLE:

> Poor Jackie. The problems of family life cause him to suffer a heart attack. Jackie dies. Fortunately, Art recovers from his stroke and now signs the deed conveying the condo to the buyers of Jackie's property. Jackie sold the condo for $150,000 and Art is pleased with this investment. His father bought the place for $20,000 30 years earlier. Art learns however, that the IRS may assess a capital gains tax on one-half of the gain in the property—Art's half. So Art faces paying a capital gains tax on $65,000 worth of gain.

How is the capital gains tax figured? In the example above, Art receives a new cost basis for Jackie's one-half of the property. This cost basis would be $75,000 ($150,000 divided in half). He takes Jackie's original basis for his one-half of the property. This cost basis would be $10,000. (Original purchase price of $20,000 divided in half.) His total cost basis is $85,000 ($10,000 plus $75,000). The property sold for $150,000, so the gain is $150,000 minus $85,000 or $65,000. This example does oversimplify the calculations somewhat. If Jackie had made improvements to the property (e.g. he remodeled the kitchen, etc.) these costs would be added to his cost basis, making the gain smaller.

These types of problems with unnecessary capital gains can be avoided by ensuring that the beneficiary receives the whole asset through some form of inheritance rather than via a joint tenancy. If Art had received the entire interest in the property via a will or trust, he would receive a cost basis equal to the value as of the date of Jackie's death on the entire condo.

Joint tenancy may, under some circumstances, be an appropriate way to hold title between husband and wife. It may cause estate tax consequences if the married couple's assets exceed the estate tax exemption amount. (We will look at estate taxes in a later chapter.) In any event, joint tenancy should be approached with great caution when considering a joint tenancy with someone other than a spouse. Joint tenancy has many perils of which the average person is unaware. Too often it is viewed as the replacement for a more effective estate plan. Other types of planning may help minimize the concerns that cause you to consider creating a joint tenancy in the first place.

Beneficiary designations are another form of informal estate planning in which many people engage without realizing the full impact it may have. For example, most persons designate beneficiaries on a life insurance policy, or an IRA. The beneficiary has no legal interest in the asset so long as the owner is alive; therefore, beneficiary designations avoid some of the pitfalls of joint tenancies.

Beneficiary designations are limited to certain types of assets. Life insurance, most deferred compensation plans (like 401(k) plans), IRAs, bank accounts, and U.S. savings bonds can have death beneficiary stipulations. Beneficiary designations can be an effective tool in planning simple estates. This form of holding title does not provide any disability protection, however, as the person named to receive the property upon death has no ability to access the asset during the owner's lifetime. Furthermore, these types of designations usually do not provide for any estate tax planning, and improper designations, especially on IRAs or deferred compensation plans, may have unwanted income tax consequences. Contingent beneficiaries may or may not be allowed. For example, on a life insurance policy, if the owner's son, named as death beneficiary, predeceases the owner, a contingent recipient (e.g. the grandchildren) can be named. On a "payable on death" bank account, however, if the son predeceased his father, the asset becomes part of the father's probate estate, as no contingencies are typically allowable. Many people do not understand this, and wrongly assume that contingent recipients are presumed.

EXAMPLE:

Bill and Hillary have one child, Chelsea. Unfortunately, Bill passes away at an early age, probably due to excessive consumption of fatty foods that gave him heart disease. The total assets that Bill and Hillary owned dwindled somewhat in the years prior to Bill's death, as the couple had large legal fees to pay defending Bill from various lawsuits. After Bill dies, Hillary makes a new will that leaves her entire estate to Chelsea, if she is living, otherwise to Chelsea's two children, Albert and Newt. Hillary has several bank accounts in her name. She designates Chelsea as a "payable on death" beneficiary on the accounts. Misfortune seems to strike in threes. Within a year after Bill's death, Chelsea meets with an unfortunate accident and dies. Hillary, heartbroken, dies three days later. Hillary's payable on death designation is now meaningless because Chelsea did not survive her. Hillary's will now controls where the accounts will go—to Newt and Albert—but her will must be probated, that is, handled through court proceedings.

Death beneficiary designations have limits as estate plans. And as mentioned above, they are useless as a tool to protect against disability or incompetency.

EXAMPLE:

> Howard has an IRA account. On the account, he has listed his wife, Mary, as his death beneficiary. His three children, Bill, Lisa, and Maggie, are listed as contingent beneficiaries. Howard suffers from Alzheimer's disease, and by age 70, no longer recognizes his family. Federal tax law requires Howard to begin taking withdrawals from his IRA this year. Mary needs to take withdrawals from Howard's IRA account, or the IRS will begin to impose penalties. Because the IRA account is in Howard's name alone, Mary cannot sign any of the paperwork necessary to request withdrawals. She has no rights as beneficiary so long as Howard is alive.

The informal estate plan of Mary and Howard has failed them. If they have not prepared a formal estate plan, Mary may be headed toward guardianship court. She may be forced to petition to become Howard's guardian.

More formal plans exist to forestall problems such as those that Mary and Howard face. For those of you who choose not to avoid the lawyer's office, tools such as trusts, powers of attorney, and their progeny can coordinate with or take the place of informal plans such as joint tenancies and beneficiary designations. Our next chapter deals with these formal planning devices.

5

Formal Planning:
Putting Your Thoughts on Paper

As Chapter 2 showed us, if you become incompetent, two questions arise. Who can make a healthcare decision on your behalf? And who can handle your financial affairs? Chapter 3 detailed the most popular approach we take to these concerns: we do nothing! Chapter 4 took the "no plan" approach of Chapter 3 and added to it some informal planning that many of us do: joint tenancies and beneficiary designations. This chapter looks at more formal ways to deal with the problem of incompetency.

The documents discussed in this chapter range from simple forms such as a living will to complex multifaceted documents like a trust. Some of the tools discussed can be "do-it-yourself" tools. Others do entail a trip to the lawyer's office. You may consider consulting an attorney for any of the documents mentioned in this chapter to be sure the documents are drafted and signed properly.

Personal and healthcare decisions are perhaps the most important of the concerns that we address in this book. If you wish to provide for a way for personal and healthcare decisions to be made on your behalf in the event of incompetency, you may choose from some basic tools. These alternatives providing the answer as to whom might make a healthcare decision are sometimes referred to as advance medical directives. Statistics show that only about 10 percent of all people entering a hospital have some form of advance medical directive. Despite the publicity generated by the "right to die," it seems as if most people still do not want to face this issue.

This seems consistent with the popularity of the "no plan" approach we discussed in Chapter 3.

If you wish to plan, however, the first type of advance medical directive to consider is a "living will." Perhaps the most poorly named legal document, a living will is nothing like a will that disposes of your property at your death. In fact, a living will has nothing whatsoever to do with your financial affairs. Simply stated, a living will is a directive to your doctor stating that you do not wish to be kept alive on life support if you are terminally ill.

In many states, the legislature created living wills by passing a statute that recognizes these documents. Often, statutory forms—suggested forms devised by the state legislature—are provided. If a statutory form exists, it may be wise to use this form. With living wills, creativity is not rewarded. While you may wish an alternative to the living will form that your state legislature provides, be aware that medical personnel will be more comfortable dealing with a statutory form. Doctors and hospitals will be more likely to honor a statutory form without undue complication for your family. If you want to put down on paper your own specific instructions, consider starting with a statutory form and adding to it, or modifying it according to your desires.

What if your state does not have a statutory form? Most stationary supply houses have generic forms of living wills that you can peruse. You can also prepare your own from scratch. If your state does not have a specific statutory form, you should see a lawyer to prepare your living will. A lawyer will know what specific items must be incorporated into your living will to be sure it is valid. For example, your state may require two witnesses or a notary public to witness your signature. You may need to have specific language in a paragraph where the witnesses say they saw you sign, that you were of sound mind, and that they are not related to you, etc. Without knowing what requirements your state sets forth, you may create an invalid document.

If your state has a suggested statutory form, you can usually obtain a copy from a stationery store, hospital, or senior center. Some of the statutory forms are "do-it-yourselfers" or can be completed with the assistance of a social worker or staff person at a senior center.

Most living will forms are one-page directives. If you look at a living will you will see that it usually does not give authority to any family member or friend to make healthcare decisions for you. It gives direction to your attending physician about life sustaining care.

Thus, the living will is a limited set of instructions. It is limited in that it does not name any person to act on your behalf. It is more severely limited in that it only deals with life sustaining care. It does not deal with more routine medical care in the event you are incompetent but not terminally or hopelessly ill.

A more comprehensive advance medical directive is a durable power of attorney for healthcare. This document is sometimes called a healthcare proxy. With this document, you appoint someone to make healthcare decisions for you if you are unable. In the power of attorney, the person you appoint is called an agent. Typically, your agent might be your spouse, or if you are single, a child, nephew or niece, or other trusted family member or friend. Most powers of attorney allow for appointment of a successor or backup agent. This person would act if your first choice is unavailable, deceased, or sick. You can usually select as many successor agents as you wish. You should always have at least one successor agent, but more than two or three backups is probably overkill.

The power of attorney for healthcare is a much broader document than a living will. It can provide for virtually any healthcare decision, whether routine or life sustaining. For example, your agent can admit you to a hospital, obtain copies of medical records from your doctor, and consent to surgery. Your agent could also terminate life support if you are hopelessly ill. Thus, it often eliminates the need for a living will because it encompasses the types of circumstances that a living will does. It can also eliminate the need for a guardian of the person. A well-drafted healthcare power should allow complete access to medical records, complying with the federal HIPAA law mentioned earlier.

The power of attorney for healthcare is a durable power, meaning that it continues until death despite the maker's subsequent incapacity. Care should be taken in using old power of attorney forms, because the form may be for a non-durable power. A non-durable power would become invalid if you became incompetent, the time when you most need it to function!

Like the living will, state statutes frequently contain suggested forms for these powers of attorney. You probably should consider using a statutory form, if one exists in your state, and modifying as needed for your wishes. Medical personnel will be more comfortable with statutory forms of the durable power.

Some states provide forms that incorporate a living will together with the designation of a healthcare agent in one document. The form may be called a "healthcare proxy" or may be entitled "living will" when in fact, it is both forms in one.

You may be able to complete a power of attorney for healthcare, especially a statutory form, on your own. If not, a good social worker or senior center staff person can help. Again, lawyers will do powers of attorney for healthcare. You may consider having one prepared by your lawyer as part of a comprehensive estate and asset protection plan.

If you want to provide for healthcare decision making according to your wishes, then you need some form of advance medical directive. A living will is often the choice for those who are single and have no relative or friend who they either would entrust or burden with these decisions. If you have trustworthy individuals willing to act on your behalf, then the power of attorney for healthcare is the better option. Either of these documents can provide peace of mind, help preserve your estate against medical bills due to a long, lingering illness, and can obviate the need for a costly, intrusive guardianship of the person. With the complexity and cost of healthcare, no estate plan is complete without considering the issue of healthcare decision-making.

A complete estate plan should also include a mechanism for someone to step in and manage your financial affairs in the event of incompetency. As noted in the previous chapter, joint tenancies or beneficiary designations may not be an effective means of planning an estate. Further, most jointly-held property, with bank accounts being the principal exception, require the consent (and signature) of all joint owners to handle, convey, or otherwise deal with the property. Reliance on joint ownership as an incapacity protection plan can be misplaced.

One of the formal means that are available to plan in advance for financial management in the event of disability is a durable power of attorney for property. This document operates much like the power of attorney for healthcare. In the property power, you appoint someone to act as your agent. Your agent can be authorized, within the provisions contained in the power, to act on your behalf in a broad range of financial matters. You can allow your agent to convey real estate, access bank accounts, engage in stock transactions, endorse and deposit checks, and sign tax returns. This power can be a very broad grant of authority: care should be exercised in selecting an appropriate agent!

The term "property" as used in this power of attorney can be misleading. You may think that a property power of attorney would allow someone to deal with your real estate only. However, property, is used here in the broad, legal sense. Property includes anything in which you have a legal interest: from real estate to bank accounts to securities, and all assets. The easiest way to look at a property power is to substitute the word "financial" for property. Thinking of this document as a "financial power of attorney" clues you in on what this tool can do for you.

The financial or property power can be effective upon signing, or it can be a "springing power." A springing power becomes effective upon the occurrence of a specific event. For example, the power could become effective upon the written determination by a physician that you can no longer manage your financial affairs. Springing powers are trickier to draft and implement. There are two points to keep in mind if you are considering a springing power of attorney. First, what event will cause the power to "spring" into life, and who is needed to cause the event to occur? If, as in our previous example, you want your power of attorney to become effective when a doctor says you are incapable, your family may have difficulty persuading a doctor to make that determination. And even if you get the doctor's report, anyone who deals with your agent under the power of attorney will require a copy of the report. Not only does this invade your privacy—the bank clerk at the neighborhood bank will know you have Alzheimer's disease if she sees a doctor's report to that effect—but you give third parties more reasons to scrutinize your power of attorney and perhaps reject it. Second, why make it a springing power? When most persons who create springing powers are asked why they had the document prepared in this fashion, it usually boils down to a fear that the person named as agent will usurp his or her rights or act wrongfully. If this were the case, wouldn't an agent who was going to misbehave be more likely to do so when you lose competency and are much less likely to stop him? In other words, suppose you name your son as agent, but make the power of attorney a springing power. You do so because you are worried your son might use the power of attorney against your wishes. If you become sick and need help, wouldn't your less-than-trustworthy son now take advantage of you? The better solution is to avoid springing powers and avoid naming untrustworthy persons as agent under any power of attorney. The best way to draft a property power of attorney is to make it effective upon signing. That way, there is no question that it is effective, and no one needs to see any physician's letters or worry about any other triggering events.

Like the durable power of attorney for healthcare, the property power is often authorized by state statute, with a suggested statutory form. Care should be taken to ensure that unwanted tax consequences do not result from the grant or exercise of a specific power by the agent, like a power to make gifts.

Unlike the living will or power of attorney for healthcare that are frequently completed by lay persons, the power of attorney for property is a document that usually requires an attorney's advice to prepare. Failure to consult with an attorney can result in bad tax consequences, or an ineffective power. Like the healthcare power, make sure that a "durable" power is created. Many forms exist for general powers of attorney. These are useless as asset protection tools because they become invalid upon loss of capacity.

Transfer agents, banks, and others in the financial world have traditionally dealt with general (non durable) powers of attorney. This leads to reluctance to deal with agents acting under durable powers of attorney. While state laws have been drafted to obviate this problem, it still seems to persist. Transfer agents or banks often erect barriers that the agent must overcome to exercise her granted powers. Sometimes having the lawyer who prepared the power place a phone call or write a concise letter can alleviate problems.

Having a lawyer prepare the power of attorney in the first place instead of deciphering a pre-printed form on your own is a good idea. Unlike the healthcare power of attorney, non-lawyers usually do not assist in preparing a property power of attorney. In fact, in most states, preparation of a power of attorney for property by a non-lawyer for you would be the unauthorized practice of law. While requiring a trip to the lawyer's office, the power of attorney for property is a simple and inexpensive document to create.

A second estate-planning tool to prevent incapacity from causing problems is the living trust.

A living trust requires three parties to be valid. The first, the settlor, is the person who creates the trust, and whose assets are placed into the trust. The second is the trustee, who manages the assets in the trust. Finally, we have the beneficiary (or beneficiaries) of the trust. These are individuals who receive the income that the assets in the trust generate, and most often have the right to withdraw some or all the assets from the trust.

A simple analogy to a trust is a corporation. Most people know what a corporation is and how it operates. Corporations have shareholders, who contribute money to the corporation when they buy stock. The settlor of a trust is like the shareholders of a corporation. A corporation also has officers and directors that manage the corporation. This is similar to the trustee of a trust. Finally, the corporation will pay dividends to its shareholders; the shareholders can also sell stock for cash at any time. Shareholders are akin to the beneficiaries of a trust.

Usually, the settlor of the trust is also the beneficiary for her life. Contingent beneficiaries are named if the settlor dies.

EXAMPLE:

> Dave Thomas creates a trust and places some of his assets into the trust. He is the settlor of the trust. His trust names himself as beneficiary. Under the terms of the trust, Dave receives all income from the trust assets and can withdraw any or all assets at any time. In his trust, Dave names his daughter Wendy as beneficiary in the event he dies. If Dave dies, Wendy is then entitled to the income and to receive the assets from the trust.

A living trust can be created in two formats: a self-declaration of trust or a trust agreement. Most people execute a self-declaration of trust, allowing themselves to be their own trustee while alive and able. Some people, especially when health is already failing, create trust agreements where a third party, typically a family member or a bank or trust company, acts as trustee.

EXAMPLE:

> When Dave Thomas created his trust, he named himself as trustee. Dave has established a self-declaration of trust.

Once the trust is signed, a person transfers certain of her assets into the trust. If a living trust holds the settlor's assets it is "funded." If a trust is funded, and then the settlor becomes incapacitated, the trust can continue to manage the assets held within the trust for her benefit, without any court intervention. In the case of a trust agreement, the third party trustee will continue financial management without interruption. In the case of a self-declaration of trust, the trust document will name a successor trustee (usually a family member, bank, or trust company) to take over as trustee and continue financial management without court intervention.

EXAMPLE:

> Dave Thomas, as settlor, creates a trust. He names himself as trustee and beneficiary. This is a self-declaration of trust. Dave names his daughter Wendy as successor trustee. Dave has a stroke and can no longer manage his financial affairs. His daughter Wendy takes over his trust and can pay his bills, protect his assets, and maintain her father with the trust income and assets. No court had to preside over the transition of trustees.

The succession of trustees in a self-declaration of trust is a confusing concept for many. The key to trustee succession is understanding that a trust, like a corporation, is a separate legal entity. A trust holds title to property, can sue and be sued, and continues even if persons associated with it become incompetent or die. You may know that there was a real Dave Thomas, who was the CEO of Wendy's, a corporation that oversees thousands of fast food restaurants. What happened when the real Dave Thomas died? Wendy's—the corporation—elected a new CEO and kept on going. Similarly, if the real Dave Thomas had become incapacitated, it would not have affected the corporation. Death or incapacity of a company CEO does not stop the corporation because it is a separate legal entity. In our example above, the trust of our fictional Dave Thomas is not affected by his stroke.

Unlike the power of attorney for property, a living trust is more readily accepted by transfer agents, banks, and real estate title companies, and fewer complications result when a successor trustee needs to assume control of the trust. One reason for this is the difference in length of existence of these two tools. Durable powers of attorney are a fairly recent invention, appearing only a few decades ago. The idea of a trust is rooted deep in English law. Trusts have been in existence for centuries. The concept of a trust was carried to America with much of the English law when our country was settled and became independent. Thus, banks, brokers, and real estate title agents have been dealing with trusts since the earliest days of formal legal systems.

A plan for management of your financial affairs is a needed addition to an overall estate planning and preservation strategy. Without proper planning, a costly and intrusive guardianship can result.

Incompetency is a common occurrence. It affects a person prior to death, making its impact even greater. Planning to minimize the disruptive nature of incompetency is an important goal of any effective estate and asset preservation approach. Tools such as living wills and powers of attorney for healthcare can deal with the important issue of healthcare decision-making. Powers of attorney for property and trusts can ease the impact of incompetency on the financial side.

Unfortunately, incompetency is often the precursor to the ultimate problem in life: death. If you have a stroke or suffer from some form of dementia, a well thought out asset protection plan will safeguard your assets and well being during those times. But what happens if you should pass away? What types of concerns do you need to address to be sure that your asset protection plan now works to better the lives of your spouse, children, or other family members who will inherit from you? Our next series of chapters looks at the second goal in asset protection planning: protection of assets upon death.

6

Probate and Other Curse Words

Our last several chapters looked at how you can protect your assets if you become incompetent. We looked at various planning options. We also looked at what happens if you fail to plan. Our next chapters turn to another goal in asset protection planning: protection of assets when you die.

When you die, a number of threats exist to shrink your hard earned dollars before they reach your spouse or children. This chapter and chapters 7, 8, 9 and 10 deal with some of these perils. You may also be concerned that settling your estate will be difficult for your family. You may have heard of horror stories where estates are tied up for months or years before the family receives inheritances. Much of the delay, cost, and annoyance of settling estates is blamed on the probate system. In this chapter we will examine the probate system, learning what it is and how it operates.

Probate is a court proceeding. Probate courts verify the validity of a deceased person's will, or if the person had no will, determine who will inherit from the decedent. The court's involvement continues until your estate is settled and inheritances are distributed to the rightful parties. In many states, probate courts also have jurisdiction over guardianships of incompetent adults and minors. So the same court that might oversee your affairs if you become incompetent could also supervise your affairs when you die.

When you die, under what circumstances must your estate be handled in the probate court? The rules on probate vary from state to state. However, virtually every state has a two-part rule on when a decedent's estate must be opened in court. Basically, your estate would be probated if, at death: (1) you own assets, titled solely in your name with no joint tenants, beneficiary designations, or trust titling, that (2) when totaled together, exceed a specific dollar value. The dollar value is the second part of the rule and it varies from state to state. In some states it is as low as $5,000; in others as high as $100,000. Once you know the number, however, that part of the rule is easily understood. It is the titling aspect that confuses people. Try to keep in mind that "solely owned" assets in the world of probate are defined as assets where there is no other legal mechanism in place in the titling of the asset for another person to directly inherit.

EXAMPLE:

Minnie Pennywise dies. At her death, she has three assets: a savings account titled jointly with her daughter, worth $100,000; a savings account that lists her son as a "payable on death" beneficiary, worth $90,000; and a checking account in her name alone with a balance of $3,500. Minnie lives in a state, which currently allows a decedent's estate to be handled without probate court if the total value of solely owned assets does not exceed $50,000. Minnie's son and daughter are both living when she passed away. Minnie's estate will not have to be probated. The two savings accounts pass directly to her son and daughter. The checking account can be accessed without court intervention.

Assuming that your estate that is solely owned is under your state's dollar limit, how does family access those assets? In most cases, state law allows for a family member to prepare and present an affidavit to the institution where the asset is held.

EXAMPLE:

Minnie Pennywise, dying with the three accounts we listed above, has a will that leaves her estate equally to her son and daughter. Minnie's daughter completes a small estate affidavit and gives it to the bank where Minnie had her checking account. The affidavit has a death certificate for Minnie attached, as well as a copy of her will. The bank will close the account and give the funds to Minnie's children.

A common misconception is that a will avoids probate. In fact, if you want your will to control disposition of your estate, in many cases your will must be probated. We already reviewed how joint tenancy or beneficiary designations, while avoiding probate, can conflict with a will.

EXAMPLE:

> George Busch has two daughters, Barbara and Millie. George has his lawyer, Dick Millhouse, prepare a will that leaves his entire estate equally to his two girls. Millie lives in the same town as George while Barbara lives out of state. George puts Millie's name on all his bank accounts as a joint tenant so she can pay his bills if he becomes sick. George dies. His estate consists of his house, worth about $125,000, titled in his name alone, his bank accounts, totaling $150,000, titled in his name and Millie's name, and a brokerage account, titled in his name alone, containing $75,000 in various securities. George's will must be probated. His probate estate will consist of his brokerage account and house, which will be split equally. His bank accounts are not part of his probate estate because Millie is a joint tenant. The bank accounts do not need to be probated because of the joint tenancy. Luckily, Millie and Barbara get along quite well, and they work things out informally between them so each will get one-half of George's total assets.

If you want to be sure that your will accurately divides your assets, and if your assets exceed the amount your state law allows you to pass without probate, then probating of your will is necessary. Many people have wills, but create joint tenancies with children or other relatives. As we have seen, joint tenancies can muddy the waters when it comes to dividing assets. It can contradict what you want your will to do.

If your estate is probated, what happens? Many stories abound in magazine articles and books about the "evils" of probate. Probate can be onerous, depending upon your state's probate laws.

Many states allow for unsupervised or independent administration of probate estates. An independent estate means that the court does not directly oversee the executor's actions. What the court will see are documents signed by all beneficiaries of the estate that each of them has looked over the executor's acts and found them acceptable.

Other states allow only court supervised estate administration. These states require an executor to seek court approval for virtually every action she might take. Direct and intrusive court supervision causes the estate to incur more costs to settle. You may wish to check with a local attorney to find out if your state allows for independent administration of probate estates. It makes for an easier and cheaper settlement of your affairs.

If independent administration is possible, the first step in probating an estate is for the attorney to prepare a petition to admit the will to probate. The attorney then files the petition and sets a date to appear before the judge. Assuming the papers are in order, the judge will enter an order admitting the will to probate and appointing the executor to act.

The executor then receives a document, called a "letter of office," from the court. With this document, he can collect the assets of the decedent. The executor opens new accounts in the name of the estate, into which he deposits the decedent's assets. The executor can sell any real estate or other assets, if necessary, at this time.

The executor must prepare an inventory and an accounting of his activities. The inventory is a list of the decedent's assets that the executor gathered together. The accounting starts with the inventory and details the income the estate earned, any assets sold and the gain or loss on sales, and all bills paid. The ending balance of the accounting is what is available to be distributed to the beneficiaries of the estate. When the estate is ready to be closed, the attorney will prepare documents, signed by each beneficiary, indicating that every beneficiary approved of the inventory and accounting, and received his or her share. Before closing the estate, the executor must be sure that he has filed or otherwise provided for all tax returns.

How long does probate take? An estate must stay open long enough for any creditors of the estate to have an opportunity to file claims. A claim is a demand to be paid from the estate. Someone can file a claim if the decedent owes her money or if the estate owes her money.

EXAMPLE:

> George Busch's will is admitted to probate. His daughter Barbara is named in the will as executor. The court appoints her to act. She receives notice in the mail of three claims being filed against George's estate. George owed money to First Kennebunkport Bank Credit Card when he died. The credit card company wants to be paid. Clinton funeral agency handled George's burial. They want to be paid the $7,000 funeral cost. Finally, George did not have a Medicare supplemental insurance policy when he died. The hospital where he was taken the night of his death is owed the balance of the bill that Medicare did not pay. The hospital notifies Barbara of its claim.

Each state has a time limit during which claims must be filed. Claims not filed during that time period are forever barred. These time limits are in place so an executor knows when it will be safe to close the estate. Once all claims are satisfied, the executor has finished all her other duties, and the claims period has elapsed, the executor can distribute the money to the beneficiaries without fear of the estate owing more. Most states provide for a six-month claims period.

Sometimes an estate will stay open longer than the claims period. If real estate needs to be sold and it is still on the market, the estate may not close. If the decedent had a business that is for sale, if a beneficiary is contesting the estate, or if the estate is involved in any other lawsuits, it may stay open. In addition, if the estate owes federal estate taxes (more about these in Chapter 9) the executor will keep the estate open until she is sure that the IRS will not contest the estate tax return.

Probate incurs costs that are paid from the estate. An executor is entitled to a fee for acting. In some states, the executor's fee is calculated as a percentage of the value of the estate. For example, a state may allow an executor administering an estate of $200,000 a fee of 2%. In this example, the fee would be $4,000. In other states, the executor must keep time records, and will be compensated based on an hourly rate. The hourly rates are modest, averaging $15 to $30 per hour. An executor may choose to waive the fee. This is most common when a relative such as a child is acting, particularly if the executor is also a beneficiary. There are also court filing fees, which are usually nominal (a few hundred dollars at most). The estate typically publishes a notice in a local newspaper to alert potential claimants of the person's death. Newspapers charge between $100 and $200 for this service. The biggest cost of probate is attorney's fees. In some states, attorneys are paid based on a percentage of the value of the estate (like an executor). In other states, the attorney bills on an hourly basis. Occasionally, an attorney will quote a flat fee for handling an estate.

If you have no will the costs for handling an estate increase. First, the fees of the attorney are typically higher, because a probate estate of a person with no will involves more work by the attorney. The attorney must prepare and file with the court additional documents to aid the court in determining who will be the heirs of the decedent. Additionally, a probate estate of a decedent who died without a will does not have an executor. The person appointed to handle the estate is called an administrator. The administrator has many similar powers to an executor, but an administrator has to post a "surety bond" with the court. This bond, purchased from an insurance company, guarantees that the administrator will not mismanage or steal from the estate. The surety bond is an additional cost born by the estate. Thus, dying without a will may cause your estate to shrink further before it reaches your heirs.

If you die without a will you are said to have an "intestate" probate estate. If you die with a will you have a "testate" probate estate. An administrator is a person whom settles an intestate estate while an executor handles a testate one. You may come across the terms "administratrix" or "executrix" in magazines or other books you read. These are simply feminine versions of the words administrator and executor.

Neither an administrator nor an executor has any powers without letters of office from the court. The mere act of naming an executor in your will does not empower him to act. The court must appoint him after a petition for probate is filed. The court can also decline to appoint your choice of executor if it finds he is unable or unsuitable. The court would look then to your second (or third) choice for an executor to appoint.

EXAMPLE:

> The late George Busch named his daughter, Barbara, as executor in his will. But Barbara has died before George, so the court cannot appoint her. George's second choice, his attorney Dick Millhouse, is currently serving a lengthy prison sentence for various white-collar crimes. The court declines to appoint Attorney Millhouse, finding him both unsuitable and unable. The third choice is George's other daughter, Millie. Millie is able and willing to act. The court enters an order appointing Millie as executor of the estate.

When preparing a will you should always have at least two and preferably three choices as executor. In the event that your first or second choice cannot act, the court will have alternates to select. In addition, just because someone is named as executor, and is able to act, does not mean he can be forced to do so. Anyone can decline to act as executor of a will. Before you name anyone in your will as executor, check with him or her to be sure he or she would be willing to do the job.

If a will names an executor and one or more backups, and all persons named are either unable or unwilling, the will is still valid. The court will appoint an administrator to handle the will. The technical term for this person is an "administrator with will annexed."

If you die intestate, how does a court pick an administrator? State law provides a pecking order of persons with preference to act. The pecking order is generally based upon degrees of kinship. Thus, a spouse has first right to ask to be administrator, followed by children, and on down the line of your relatives. If you have no relatives or none that wish to act, then a public official such as a public administrator will handle your estate.

The same degrees of kinship determine who will inherit from you if you die intestate. It is a common misconception is that if you die without a will the state takes your property—not true! Spouses and children come first as your heirs. If you do not have a living spouse or any living children, other lineal descendants, such as grandchildren or great grandchildren are next in line. If you have no spouse or descendants, state laws usually go up your family tree to parents and brothers and sisters, or nieces, nephews, and other collateral relatives. State law governs intestacy. The statutes will search your family tree looking for any relatives. Only if you have absolutely no living relatives does your estate pass to the state in which you live. In-laws are not considered under state statutes, so if you have no blood relatives, but your sister-in-law is still alive, she is not your heir.

If you die without a will the old adage is that the state has provided one for you. State intestacy statutes will pick your heirs. Add to that the fact that statutes will designate who will handle your estate as administrator. Top this off with the additional costs of an intestate estate and you have three big advantages that a well-drafted simple will give you. With a will you: (1) determine the beneficiaries of your estate; (2) name a trusted person to act as executor; (3) keep the costs down and preserve more of your estate for your beneficiaries.

Seventy percent of all Americans do not even have a simple will. The most common estate plan is the same as the most common incompetency protection plan: the "do-nothing" approach. Probating a will may not be the most efficient way to handle your estate. In the following chapters we will look at some other methods to pass property to your family without the inconvenience and costs of probate. Probate of a will is still far superior to an intestate probate estate. A will is the most basic of estate planning tools. As we will see in the upcoming chapters, wills still provide one of the tools you must have in any estate and asset protection plan, no matter how sophisticated.

7

When Can You Trust Trusts?

In Chapter 5, we discussed trusts in some detail. Trusts are one tool you can use to avoid the problems of incompetency. A trust will help protect assets if you become disabled. When you incorporate a trust into your asset protection plan, it can also act as a will substitute if you should pass away.

The last chapter looked at probate. One of the ways you can avoid probate is using a trust to pass assets at your death. Exactly how does settling an estate through a trust differ from probating an estate?

To understand how your trust would be settled when you die, and how this differs from probate, we need to first understand the mechanics of how a trust works. As we learned in chapter five, a trust needs three parties to be valid: 1) the settlor (the one who creates the trust and puts assets into it); 2) the trustee (the one who manages the trust); 3) one or more beneficiaries (the one or ones for whose benefit the trust assets are held).

When the creator of a trust dies, two of the three parties to the trust may change. First, the beneficiaries of the trust usually change upon death.

EXAMPLE:

> John Smith creates a trust, naming himself as its beneficiary for his life. The trust states that when John dies, the beneficiaries become his two sons, Plymouth and Rock.

Second, the trustee of the trust may also change. In Chapter 5, we looked at the difference between a self-declaration of trust and a trust agreement. Depending on whether the trust is a trust agreement or a self-declaration of trust, the document may designate a new trustee to take over.

EXAMPLE:

John Smith creates a self-declaration of trust. This document names John as trustee. In his trust, he names his son Rock to be successor trustee upon his death. John dies. Rock should now take over managing the trust.

The third party to the trust does not change: the settlor! Why is this important? The settlor is typically the only one who can revoke or change the trust. A trust normally becomes irrevocable at the settlor's death, that is, the terms of the trust become fixed. This ensures that the settlor's wishes will be carried out, and that no one can change the plan.

EXAMPLE:

John Smith dies. His trust leaves 40% of his estate to his son Plymouth and 60% to his son Rock. John chose to leave less to Plymouth because he did various things throughout John's life that disappointed him. Rock is successor trustee upon John's death. Plymouth tries to convince Rock to give him more of the estate, but Rock cannot change the trust. John's wishes will be carried out.

The change in parties to the trust is the key in understanding how a trust works to distribute an estate upon death. A trust avoids probate because there is still a trustee alive and able to manage the trust even after the settlor's death. A trust also acts as a will substitute because it names new beneficiaries upon the settlor's death. Let's look first at how the trust avoids probate.

Simply stated, a trust avoids probate because assets are titled in the trust, and not in the settlor's name. Whether you would create a self-declaration of trust that names a successor you as settlor, or a trust agreement, where a third party is already in place as trustee, your demise does not affect the viability of the trust.

EXAMPLE:

> John Smith creates a self-declaration of trust. Shortly after he signs the trust, he changes the title to all his assets. His bank accounts, mutual funds, and house title all now read, "John Smith, trustee, The John Smith Declaration of Trust dated July 26, 2004." John dies. The trustee of the John Smith Declaration of Trust is dead, but the trust itself is not. John's trust names his son Rock as successor trustee. Rock presents some documentation to each place where John had an account (the most noteworthy document being John's death certificate). Rock re-titles the accounts: "Rock Smith, trustee, The John Smith Declaration of Trust dated July 26, 2004."

EXAMPLE:

> Bill Jones creates a trust agreement, naming his son Fred as trustee for him. Shortly after signing the trust, Bill re-titled his accounts: "Fred Jones, trustee, The Bill Jones Trust Agreement dated August 25, 2004." Bill dies. Fred is already trustee and can continue to handle the accounts.

In both examples above, the death of the settlor did not cause the trust to "die." With a trust agreement, nothing changes. With a declaration of trust, each account holder needs some evidence of the successor trustee and his right to take over. The most important document is a copy of a death certificate, attested to by an appropriate county official, stating that the settlor is in fact, deceased.

If you create a trust, whether a self-declaration or trust agreement, your document will require the trustee to file tax returns. Often, the trustee will file your last personal tax return. The trustee may also be required to file one or more trust tax returns. The living trust, whether a self-declaration of trust or trust agreement is an income tax neutral tool. It does not increase nor decrease your income tax liability. Most often, the living trust uses your social security number as its tax identifying number. This makes tax returns easy during your life, as all tax reporting is entered onto the same tax return that individuals file.

When the settlor of a trust dies, the trust can no longer use a social security number. A person's social security number "dies" with him. The trustee must acquire a new tax identification number from the Internal Revenue Service. The trustee can do this himself by filing IRS form SS-4, or he can ask his accountant or attorney to file the form on his behalf. The trustee may also call the IRS and have the number assigned over the phone. Whether by mail or over the phone, the IRS will assign a new identification number to the trust that must be used on all accounts after the settlor's demise.

When a settlor dies and a successor trustee takes over under a declaration of trust, the successor trustee must provide the new identifying number to each account holder when he re-titles accounts.

EXAMPLE:

> John Smith dies. John Smith's son, Rock, takes over for John as successor trustee under John's declaration of trust. In addition to a death certificate and any other required documentation, all account holders will need to know the new tax identifying number for the account. John's trust has an account at First National Bank. Rock changes the account registration from: "John Smith, trustee, The John Smith Declaration of Trust dated July 25, 2004, Tax ID # 000-00-0000" to "Rock Smith, trustee, The John Smith Declaration of Trust dated July 26, 2004, Tax ID# 00-00000000."

The trustee will have certain duties to fulfill once the settlor of the trust is deceased. Often, the trust document itself spells out what many of the trustee's duties are. Typically, the trust requires that costs of last illness, funeral, any claims or other bills that the settlor owed at death be paid first. Thus, once the trustee has in his possession all the assets of the trust, he or she can begin to pay the bills.

A trustee needs to keep careful records of the assets collected and bills paid. The trust may specifically state (or if the trust is silent, state law will require) that the trustee after the settlor's death prepare an inventory. The inventory is a listing of the assets of the trust, valued as of the date of the settlor's death. The trustee will also have to prepare accountings. An accounting is a record of all receipts and expenditures. Normally, accountings are prepared on an annual basis, with a final accounting given at the time the trust is terminated and all assets distributed.

The inventory and accountings will be useful in filing the trust's tax returns. In addition, each beneficiary of the trust is entitled to receive the inventory and accountings, and the trustee will have to forward copies to all. While this may seem complicated, in many cases the inventory and accounting is easily created. If you think of the inventory as a list of "what you start with," and use a checkbook register as a basis for a great deal of the information contained in the accounting, it becomes easier to manage.

Assuming the trustee has gathered the assets, paid the bills, and filed tax returns, what next? The trust at this point may be terminated and distributed, may continue to be held as a trust for a new group of beneficiaries, or may be partially distributed and partially held as a trust. The trust document tells the trustee what he must do next. The instructions to the trustee relate to the change in another of the parties to the trust: the beneficiaries.

The smooth transition of trustees, and the titling of assets in trust allow a trust to continue after a settlor's death, avoiding probate. The designation of successor beneficiaries after the settlor dies allows the trust to act as a substitute for a will. A trust can be as detailed as a will in determining who will inherit your estate.

The simplest of trusts will distribute its assets after the settlor's final bills are paid. A trust can also name contingent beneficiaries who will inherit a share of the trust originally designated to a beneficiary who is now deceased. Specific bequests can be made, just like a will.

EXAMPLE:

John Smith dies. His trust leaves a specific bequest of $2,000 to his favorite niece, May, and then divides the rest of the trust assets equally between his two sons: Rock and Plymouth. Plymouth predeceased John, but the trust further states that should he not survive John, his ½ share passes to Plymouth's two children.

In creating a trust, you may want to assume that children or other younger relatives will surely survive you. You may initially think only of one class of beneficiaries. Better drafting of the trust results in a plan like the example above where contingent beneficiaries are named in case a primary beneficiary dies first.

A trust can also be drafted to continue as a trust for a second group of beneficiaries after the settlor's death. Persons naming minors as beneficiaries should not have a trust that would distribute assets directly to a minor! The trust can either place assets into the hands of the parent, guardian, or other appropriate adult on behalf of the child, or can hold the share in trust under the control of the trustee.

EXAMPLE:

John Smith dies. His trust leaves ½ of his estate to son, Plymouth, but he has predeceased him. His trust then names Plymouth's children to inherit their father's share. The trust will hold the shares of Plymouth's children, who are age 10 and 6, until age 21. The trust further states, however, that the trustee can use the shares created for these children to pay for their support, education and other specified needs.

Youth may not be the only reason to hold assets in trust. Sometimes, the settlor may believe that the beneficiaries, even though adults, are not wise or mature handlers of money. The funds in the trust can continue to be held for the beneficiaries long after reaching age 21. A trust can also protect assets from problems that may haunt a beneficiary. Refer to Chapter 10 for more information about this.

Occasionally, a beneficiary may be disabled. Thus, the settlor may want the trust to continue after his death so that a responsible person can handle the funds that the settlor wants to leave to the disabled beneficiary. Sometimes, disabled persons receive the assistance of various state and federal programs such as Medicaid, other types of public aid, subsidized housing and more. Receiving an inheritance outright or even in a trust designed to support the disabled person can jeopardize such aid. Many states allow the creation of "supplemental needs" trusts. These trusts contain specific language that authorizes the trustee to supplement the aid that a disabled person receives from various public sources without risking forfeiture of the aid. A supplemental needs trust can be created within a self-declaration of trust or trust agreement. Putting all these ideas together, a very flexible document can be created.

EXAMPLE:

Jack Cassity dies. His self-declaration of trust names his daughter, Shirley Johnson, to act as successor trustee. Shirley takes over after Jack's death. She acquires a new tax identification number from the IRS and retitles Jack's accounts into her name as successor trustee. Shirley pays Jack's funeral bill, unreimbursed medical bills, and other miscellaneous outstanding debts that Jack had. Then Shirley looks at the provisions in Jack's trust that tell her who receives an inheritance. The trust first states that 1/3 of the trust assets go to each of Jack's three children: Shirley herself, and brothers Jack Jr., and David. David is dead and Jack Jr. is developmentally disabled. Shirley looks further at her father's trust and finds that she can take her 1/3 share now. She makes this distribution to herself. The trust provides that David's 1/3 share goes to his two children. One is age 18 and the other is 14. But Jack's trust allows Shirley to keep these shares until David's children are each 21. Jack's trust further allows Shirley to pay for support, education, and other needs of David's children from their shares. One is entering State College and needs money for tuition. Shirley is able to pay this from that child's share. Finally, Jack's trust sets up a supplemental needs trust for Jack Jr.'s share. Jack Jr. will continue to reside at Partridge Acres, the residential facility where the state pays for most of his care. Shirley uses Jack Jr.'s share of the trust to purchase clothing, a TV set, and several trips for him.

One of the most important choices to make in crafting a living trust is the naming of trustees. The successor trustee in a self-declaration of trust (or the initial trustee in a trust agreement) is charged with many responsibilities. In the previous example, fictional Shirley Johnson had to gather assets together and pay bills. She had to manage funds for brother David's children until age 21. She had to manage a share of the trust for brother Jack Jr. for the rest of his life.

What if Shirley had a full time career or children of her own to care for? When does administering a trust become too burdensome?

Most often, in creating a trust, you would look to family members to act as trustee during the time the trust is being settled. Obviously, if a family member is to act, care must be taken to select an appropriate person. It goes without saying that a spendthrift, unstable or immature person makes a poor trustee!

It may be less obvious that busy lifestyles may make a person a poor choice as well. If in our example above Shirley is a busy physician with a private practice, she may not be the best trustee despite her intelligence and good sense.

Sometimes, the creator of a trust will turn to banks or trust companies to act as trustee. A bank or trust company can be an excellent choice under many circumstances. If a settlor has no reliable family members, family members who are all out of the area, or who lead busy personal lives, a corporate trustee may be just the thing. A corporate trustee also works well when beneficiaries do not get along, if a trust is complex or designed to last a long time after the settlor's death, or the settlor has an extensive estate with holdings scattered about. The corporate trustee may also have expertise to manage a well thought out investment plan and be more cognizant of tax implications of settling an estate than family. The professionals who handle trusts for their livelihood can provide knowledgeable assistance; they will not be swayed by personal issues or a fractious family, and play a big role in preserving an estate against erosion due to contests of the trust in court, mismanagement, and taxation.

The corporate trustee will charge a fee for services. This results in the trust being more expensive to settle than if a family member were to serve. Many settlors have found the fee to be well worth the trade-off for peace of mind and the unburdening of family. If a bank or trust company is named as successor to the settlor as trustee under a declaration of trust, they normally charge no fee until they begin to act.

You would need to give careful thought to choice of trustee. With the right person (or corporation) in place as trustee or successor trustee, the living trust can be the cornerstone of many estate and asset protection plans. It combines flexibility with probate avoidance into an approach that makes sense for many. As we saw in Chapter 5, it can help overcome the problems that incompetency causes. Chapter 9 and 10 will tell us how trusts can help minimize estate taxes and protect assets against a myriad of challenges to an estate plan and its beneficiaries. As we will see still later on, the living trust, sometimes combined with other types of related trusts, can help protect the estate from depletion due to long-term healthcare costs.

As an estate plan, the living trust is a more expensive and complex tool than a will and a power of attorney. Is a trust necessarily the superior plan? We will compare the living trust to a will. Our next chapter examines the pros and cons of each estate plan, offering a balanced look at these two common formal ways to settle an estate.

8

Death and Taxes: Part I Comparing Probate with Settling a Living Trust

Probating of a will or administering a trust are the two primary methods to formally settle an estate when someone dies. Much of the process is the same regardless of which method is used. Whether your assets are being passed via a will or a trust, someone has to collect those assets, pay any bills, file any tax returns, and distribute the estate.

Differences exist between the two methods. A living trust may be less expensive to settle than a probate estate. An executor of a will operates under court supervision, while a trustee of a trust does not. Variations also arise in some of the characteristics and attributes of each approach. Some of these differences may make creating a living trust more attractive than a will or vice versa. One attribute of a living trust is you have a greater sense of privacy in the settling of the estate. When a will is probated, a file is created at the local courthouse. Court files are public record. If you die, anyone could easily find your probate file and learn much about you. The probate file contains the names and addresses of your heirs and beneficiaries, a value of your estate, and a complete copy of your will. This file may also include a copy of the inventory and any accountings filed by the executor.

EXAMPLE:

Beth Marshall dies with an estate consisting of bank accounts, mutual funds, and a house, with a total value of about $300,000. Beth had a will which is filed with the court in the county where she lived. The court appoints her niece, Betty Marshall, as executor. Betty files an inventory and accounting with court before she finalizes the estate. Beth's nosy neighbor, Mr. Bickerly, has a free day, and takes a ride to the courthouse. He spends some time enjoyably reading Beth's probate file.

If you have a trust, no court files are created. No court is usually involved in settling a trust estate. There is no easily accessible source of financial and family information about you, nor is there a copy of the trust available for public inspection. However, a trust is not completely private. Copies of the trust will be required by each place where you had an account or asset. The copy of the trust provided can delete information about the death beneficiaries of the trust. No inventory or accounting of the trust is in any place to which the public can easily obtain access.

EXAMPLE:

Mary Lee dies. Mary had created a declaration of trust naming her niece, Roberta Lee, as successor trustee. Mary's trust held three assets: a bank account, a mutual fund, and a house. When Roberta takes over as successor trustee, she sends a current copy of the trust to the bank and mutual fund company. The copy deletes the beneficiaries of the trust to protect Mary's privacy. Additionally, when Roberta sells Mary's house, she provides the same abbreviated copy of the trust to the title company who will insure title to the house for the new owners.

Filing for probate of a will requires that all persons who are your heirs receive notice. An heir is someone who inherits by law from you if you die with no will or other estate plan. An heir may or may not be a beneficiary of an estate. A beneficiary is an individual or charity that is named in a will or trust to receive assets from the estate.

EXAMPLE:

Larry Davis is a widower with three children: Debbie, John, and Bill. Larry had a will that leaves his entire estate to Debbie and John. Under the laws of the state where Larry lives, Debbie, John, and Bill are his heirs. Only Debbie and John are beneficiaries.

The requirement that an heir be given notice can cause confusion, hard feelings, and sometimes, will contests. Persons who are an heir but not a beneficiary are entitled to copies of the will. They also have rights to contest a will or to demand formal proof of its validity. When a trust is being settled, there normally is no requirement that heirs receive notice. This can sometimes avoid the problems and confusion of the notice requirements of probate.

EXAMPLE:

Edward Fernwell has no children or spouse, and his two sisters are deceased. Some of his nephews and nieces have also died before him. He wants to leave his estate to a few favorite nieces. If he had a will that was probated, notice might be given to remote relatives such as great nephews and nieces. With a trust, only the named beneficiaries of the trust automatically get a copy.

A trust is not completely safe from prying eyes. If you have a trust, and a contest is filed against it, its terms may become public through the court file of the estate contest. However, a trust is generally less vulnerable to attack via an estate contest than a will may be.

Estate contests can be filed on many grounds. The two most common reasons for instituting an estate contest are lack of capacity or undue influence. A lawsuit based upon lack of capacity alleges that when you made your will or trust, you did not understand what you were doing when you signed it. A suit founded upon undue influence asserts that someone pressured you into signing the trust or will.

The filing of a will contest is fairly easy. A probate case is already in progress, so the estate contest can be filed in probate court. To contest a trust requires the filing of a separate lawsuit. Usually, the costs to pursue a trust contest are greater than a will contest. Neither type of contest is easy to win. To prove that you lacked capacity or were unduly influenced, after your death, is not an easy task. Many will contests are filed and settled, as settlement is often less expensive for the estate than defending the suit. Both wills and trusts can have added protection against these kinds of suits by adding certain clauses to discourage them. (More about those clauses in Chapter 10.) A trust is also less vulnerable to attack in some states, as the standards of proof required to overturn a trust are greater than those to override a will.

Estates are also vulnerable to attacks by your creditors. Both trusts and wills are subject to claims of creditors of the decedent. Usually, a trust, like a will, contains language that obligates the trustee to pay claims before distributing the estate. One advantage a probated will can have over a trust estate is the length of time during which unknown creditors must step forward to file a claim against your estate. Typical state statutes require an unknown creditor of a decedent file a claim within six months of the opening of a probate estate. If the claim is filed late, it is barred forever. Many states provide longer time periods to file claims against non-probated estates. A typical statute can allow two years to file a claim against a trust. The trustee who wants to distribute a trust prior to the claims period must take great care to avoid being liable for a claim presented after distribution but before the expiration of the claims period. A receipt that includes a refunding agreement is used to protect the trustee.

EXAMPLE:

> Davy Jones creates a self-declaration of trust that names his son, Michael, as successor trustee. Davy's three children, Michael, Peter, and Micky, are equal beneficiaries of the trust should Davy pass away. Davy dies, and Michael takes over as successor trustee. Six months later, Michael believes that he has paid any bills of which he is aware. But the state where Michael and Davy live has a two-year limitations period on claims against trusts. Michael would like to terminate and distribute the trust, but worries about his liability if a creditor he did not know of comes forward in the next year and a half. Michael distributes the trust, but has each of the three beneficiaries (himself included) sign an agreement that if a valid claim arises within the two year period, each beneficiary agrees to pay his proportionate share.

Another way in which a living trust can differ from a probate estate is the court supervision over money left to minors. When you create a trust, you can place language in the trust directing a successor trustee to retain the shares of minor beneficiaries within the trust. The trustee then manages the funds without court intrusion. This approach is especially attractive when leaving an inheritance to minor children. The alternative to a trust for management of a child's estate is a court appointed guardian or conservator. The guardian or conservator must report to the court periodically, and cannot invest or spend funds without court approval. The guardian usually must post a surety bond, purchased from an insurance company, to guarantee that he will not mismanage or defraud the child. With a trust, the court involvement and the issuance of a surety bond are eliminated. The trustee, who is surely someone in whom you have confidence, can exercise independent yet prudent judgment in managing the minor's funds. The trustee is obligated to act reasonably. If your trustee mismanages or defrauds a child, he or she can be held liable for the damage caused.

EXAMPLE:

Beth Swan is a single mother with a four-year-old child named Kathryn. Beth creates a self-declaration of trust that names her sister, Ann, as successor trustee. Beth meets an unfortunate end. Ann manages the trust for Kathryn's benefit, following the instructions Beth laid out in the document. The trust supports Kathryn, pays for her medical care, and even for her college education before it terminates and pays out the remaining balance to her when she reaches age 25.

Trusts for minors need not terminate at the age of majority (18 or 21, depending on the state). A trust can continue for as long as you desire, subject only to some technical limitations designed to prohibit perpetual trusts. Trust provisions for minors are not limited to children. Many a grandparent has provided for a grandchild or two with trust provisions within a trust estate plan. Even nieces, nephews and others can be dealt with in this manner.

The trust eliminates the need for a surety bond of a guardian for minors. It also eliminates the need for a surety bond that probate courts can require of an executor or administrator of a probate estate. Depending on the size of the estate, the cost of a surety bond ranges from several hundred to several thousand dollars. A trust can save the estate from this expense.

Another expense that can be avoided is the need for probate in more than one state. If you die owning real estate in a state other than your state of residence, an additional probate estate may be required. Probate required in states other than the state of residence of a decedent is referred to as "ancillary probate." The usual reason for ancillary probate is out-of-state real estate.

EXAMPLE:

> Jack Jackson dies with a simple will as his estate plan. Jack owns a home in New York, his state of residence, but also has a summer cottage in Vermont and a winter getaway in Florida. His beneficiaries may have to deal with three probate estates: one in New York, and ancillary probate estates in Vermont and in Florida.

Another set of differences between probate and settling a living trust arise in how federal income taxes are filed. After you die, but before your estate is distributed, assets in the estate may generate income. The income must be reported to the IRS, and, if necessary, taxes will be paid. Income reported by an estate, whether a probate estate or a trust estate, quickly rises through the federal tax brackets to be taxed at higher rates than individuals. Most accountants recommend that the estate not pay any taxes owed, but that the income generated be distributed to the beneficiaries and taxed to them. Smaller estates often have expenses exceeding income, and an estate can show a loss in any given year.

Two basic differences exist on how income or loss is treated depending on whether the estate is probated or not. First, a trust typically must use a calendar year for its tax year, ending on December 31st. A probate estate can elect a tax year that ends 12 months after the date of death.

EXAMPLE:

> Don Daily dies on October 12th. If Don had a trust, the trust would have to file a tax return for the year ending December 31st. If the estate was not completed by the end of the year, the trust would file another return for the year ending the following December. If Don had a probate estate instead, the estate could elect to file a return for the year ending the following September 30th. This may eliminate the need for a second tax return if the estate can be finalized within 12 months.

Second, if an estate shows a loss during time of administration, the loss can be passed forward to the beneficiaries of a probate estate. A trust usually cannot pass losses to beneficiaries.

EXAMPLE:

> Don Daily dies, and his two children, Jennie and Herman inherit his estate equally. Don had an estate of $200,000, which generated income of $5500 prior to distribution. The estate had expenses of $7500. If Don's estate was being settled in probate, each of his children may have a $1,000 loss to deduct on his or her individual return ($5500—$7500 divided by two children). If Don's estate was a trust, this loss could not be taken.

While the tax issues and other issues such as ancillary probate, surety bonds, minors in estate plans, claims, privacy, and estate contests highlight differences between trusts and wills, one area where similarities abound is the role of trustee versus executor. Whether your estate is handled by a trustee under a trust, or an executor under a will, most of the duties and obligations are the same. The trustee/executor must collect the estate, pay bills and be responsible for distributions. Inventory and accounting records must be kept. Investing the estate's assets prior to distribution must be done prudently.

The law classifies both a trustee and an executor as a "fiduciary." A fiduciary has an obligation to take great care in handling money that does not belong to him. The main difference between trustee and executor is who oversees each. A judge from probate court supervises an executor. The reports the executor files with the court are scrutinized and approved. The beneficiaries may also exercise their rights if they believe the executor has acted improperly. They have this right in addition to the protection of court examination. With a trust, no court supervision is in place. It falls upon the beneficiaries personally to take appropriate action if they believe the trustee has acted improperly.

Without a court involved, a trust is the less costly means to settle an estate. There are four categories of expenses in settling an estate. A trust is more economical than a will in two of the four.

First, the fiduciary of the estate, whether trustee or executor, is entitled to a fee. Except in some states, where the amount of the fee is set by statute, most executors and trustees are permitted fees based upon the amount of work they do. Because the jobs of trustee and executor are similar, the amount of fee each could charge is also similar. When the person acting as executor or trustee is a family member and perhaps a beneficiary as well, he or she will often waive the right to fees.

The second type of expense is professionals, other than an attorney, who assist in settling an estate. The trustee or executor may retain an accountant to prepare tax returns. A real estate broker may be used to sell a home or other real estate in the estate. All the assets of the estate must be valued for the inventory. Sometimes valuation requires the assistance of a licensed appraiser who charges a fee for her services. The aid these professionals provide varies based upon the nature of the assets in the estate rather than whether the estate is probated or not.

A third category of costs is those costs the court imposes. A filing fee is paid to open a probate estate. Other miscellaneous fees are charged by the court system to obtain certain documentation from the clerk of the court. While typically modest (usually no more than a few hundred dollars), these costs are not present when settling a trust.

The fourth area of cost in settling an estate is the fee an attorney may charge for helping the executor or trustee. This is one area where settling a trust instead of probating a will may substantially reduce costs. An attorney may be consulted when settling a trust. Because no court is involved, the attorney's time is most often limited to basic consultation and review of documents. Attorney time is much more extensive in probating a will. The attorney must prepare documents for the court. He must make several appearances in court to present the documents and advise the court as to various matters of the estate.

Some states allow an attorney to charge a fee based upon the value of the probate estate. Others require that the attorney fee be based upon the time spent and the nature of services provided.

Attorney fees can be reduced by selecting an executor or trustee who is willing and able to do much of the work whether probating an estate or settling a trust. If you pick an executor or trustee who handles the correspondence, manages the estate checkbook, and interacts directly with other professionals such as the accountant, appraiser and broker, then the attorney's time can be minimized. Unfortunately, the opposite is also true.

EXAMPLE:

> Chris Crow creates a self-declaration of trust naming her favorite niece, Raven, as successor trustee. Chris dies. Raven, who lives across the country from Chris, is very busy, working two jobs to support her family, and a few months pass before she shows up at the offices of the family attorney, Lee Baily. Raven drops off a shopping bag full of bills and other mail collected from Chris' house, and tells Lee to handle the estate. Raven then flies out of town. Because Raven is busy and out of town, Lee does all the trust administration. Lee retains a real estate broker to sell the house. He hires an accountant. He sets up the estate checking account and obtains Raven's authorization to pay the bills. Lee's final bill for services as an attorney is not much different from the amount he would have charged had Chris' estate been probated.

A competent executor can handle an estate more efficiently than a busy, disinterested, or otherwise incompetent trustee. On the other hand choosing a competent person will generally allow a trust to reduce the costs of an attorney who is called upon to help.

The following chart compares probate estates versus settling a living trust. Boldface type indicates which particular plan has the advantage.

	LIVING TRUST	PROBATE NO WILL	PROBATE WILL
Privacy	More private	Less	Less
Notice to Heirs	Not Required	Required	Required
Estate Contests	More Difficult to Do	Easier to Do	Easier to Do
Creditor Claims	Longer Time Period	Shorter Time Period	Shorter Time Period
Minors	Use trust to handle	Court supervised	Court supervised
Surety Bond Requirement	Not Required	Required	May be required
Ancillary Probate	No	May be required	May be required
Taxable Year	Calendar Year	Flexible	Flexible
Loss to Beneficiary on Tax Return	No	Yes	Yes
COSTS			
COURT FEE	No	Yes	Yes
FIDUCIARY FEE	Yes	Yes	Yes
Fiduciary fee may be waived by family member or other			
PROFESSIONAL FEES	Yes	Yes	Yes
ATTORNEY FEES	Lower	Highest	Higher

9

Death and Taxes: Part II Understanding the Federal Estate and Gift Tax System

The federal government may tax your estate when you die. The federal government may also tax certain gifts you may make during life. The laws of the federal estate and gift tax system are complex. Detailed planning to avoid these taxes, beyond a basic understanding of the rules, is outside the scope of this book. However, the basic rules of the federal estate and gift tax system do merit at least a cursory examination.

Of primary importance is to understand when a transaction incurs estate or gift tax. The rules this chapter explores assume one important fact: that if you are passing an estate or making gifts, you are a U.S. citizen, and so is your spouse. The federal estate and gift tax system has different rules for non-citizens. To plan an estate for someone who is not a citizen or has a non-citizen spouse entails an entirely distinct approach. If you are in this situation, you need to consult closely with an estate-planning attorney or accountant; failure to consider the non-citizen rules can have significant tax consequences.

Another complication in place is the recent change to the estate and gift tax law. The amount a person can pass estate tax-free is rising, from $1,000,000 in 2001, to $3,500,000 in 2009. In 2010, there is no estate tax as the amount that can be passed tax-free is unlimited. In 2011, however, the estate tax exemption returns to $1,000,000. For U.S. citizens, estate and gift taxation becomes a concern only when total wealth exceeds the federal exemption equivalent. For purposes of this chapter, we will assume a $1,000,000 exemption, but realize that this number will change over time.

While the finer points of the law can be intricate, the federal estate and gift tax system has only one basic rule:

> A U.S. citizen can pass, either by lifetime gift, or by an estate passing at his or her death, an amount equal to the exemption equivalent. The estate and gift tax is a unified system, meaning gifts made during life reduce the amount that can be given away at death. The government imposes a tax only when the exemption equivalent is exceeded.

Applying the basic rule allows you to pass up to $1,000,000, whether by gift or by death, before the federal government collects a tax.

EXAMPLE:

> Alphonse Smith gives his son, Theo, a gift of $100,000. This is the first gift Alphonse has ever made. Applying this amount to Alphonse's lifetime exemption means that he now has only $900,000 left [$1,000,000 exemption less $100,000 gift]. Assuming that he makes no more gifts, he can leave up to $900,000 tax free to the beneficiaries of his estate when he dies.

This first example is somewhat incorrect as it ignores one of the exceptions to the estate and gift tax basic rule. As you might guess, every legal rule has at least one exception. The basic estate and gift tax rule has two:

> Exception Number One: A person can make gifts of up to $12,000 per year, per recipient, without reducing his or her lifetime exemption equivalent. A gift of $12,000 or less is known as an "annual exclusion gift." (Note: this amount is scheduled to be indexed for inflation in $1,000 increments.)

Exception Number Two: A person can give an unlimited amount to his or her spouse, whether by lifetime gift, or at death. This is known as the "unlimited marital deduction."

Applying Exception Number One to the previous example gives us a more complete picture of what truly occurred from a tax standpoint:

EXAMPLE:

Alphonse Smith, having made no previous gifts, gives $100,000 to his son, Theo. Alphonse can give up to $12,000 per year to Theo, so the amount the gift reduces his lifetime exemption is $88,000 [$100,000 gift less $12,000 annual exclusion]. Alphonse's lifetime exemption remaining is now $912,000 [$1,000,000 less $88,000].

The annual exclusion is based on a calendar year. With the start of a new year, another exclusion becomes available. Splitting and timing a gift may make a difference in how the gift impacts a person's tax situation.

EXAMPLE:

Alphonse Smith wants to give son Theo $100,000. Alphonse gives Theo $50,000 in cash in December and another $50,000 next January. The first gift results in a reduction of Alphonse's lifetime exemption of $38,000 [$50,000 less the $12,000 annual exclusion]. The second gift also reduces Alphonse's lifetime total available by $38,000 as he could give another $12,000 to Theo after December 31st. Totaling the two gifts, Alphonse has reduced his lifetime exemption equivalent to $924,000 [$38,000 from the first gift plus $38,000 from the second gift, subtracted from the $1,000,000].

Spouses each have $12,000 per year annual exclusions. If a spouse joins in a gift, up to $24,000 per year per recipient can be made without gift tax consequences. Using your spouse to make gifts together with you, as well as timing gifts, can minimize or avoid reducing your lifetime exemption.

EXAMPLE:

Alphonse Smith wants to give his son Theo $96,000. Alphonse and his wife Annabelle together give Theo $24,000 per year in each of the next four calendar years. Alphonse and Annabelle have not affected either of their lifetime $1,000,000 exclusions.

The second exception to the gift and estate tax rule is easy to understand. Gifts and bequests to spouses have no tax impact. The unlimited marital deduction, put into place over a decade ago, reflected the distaste Congress had for taxing widows and widowers. It also allows for transfers of assets between spouses without much worry about recordkeeping.

EXAMPLE:

Jane Doe has total assets of $1,800,000. She marries John. John brings into the marriage his good looks, but no money. After their wedding day, Jane transfers $100,000 from her bank account into John's name. Jane then dies, and her will leaves her remaining $1,700,000 to her new groom. Jane's gift of $100,000 and her bequest of $1,700,000 to John have no estate and gift tax consequences.

Combining both exceptions to the basic estate and gift tax rule affords you a great deal of flexibility in doing tax planning.

EXAMPLE:

Jane Doe, a $1,200,000 well-to-do maiden, marries pauper John, who has nary a dime. Jane has two children from her first marriage, Ben and Jerry. After marrying John, Jane transfers $100,000 from her bank account to him. Jane then transfers another $240,000 to Ben and Jerry, in $12,000 per year increments to each over the next 10 years. Jane dies, leaving the $860,000 she has left of her assets to John. John, broken hearted, dies shortly thereafter. His will leaves his estate to Ben and Jerry. John has the $100,000 Jane gave him 10 years ago and the $860,000 he inherited from her. He passes this $960,000 to Ben and Jerry. Neither Jane nor John nor their estates pay any gift or estate tax as a result of any of these transactions.

Exception Number Two, the unlimited marital deduction makes tax planning seem awfully easy. When making a will or trust, most people want to leave everything to a spouse. If the spouse dies first, the typical will or trust would then leave the estate to children or other beneficiaries. With the unlimited marital deduction, isn't this a good strategy?

If you have an estate valued under the exemption amount (for our purposes here, $1,000,000), it may very well be a good scheme. When an estate exceeds the exemption amount, it may trigger estate taxation. The typical estate plan of—"all to my spouse if he or she is living, otherwise to my children"—takes advantage of the unlimited marital deduction. The problem is that this wastes one spouse's lifetime exemption equivalent. Thus, if you have an estate of over $1,000,000 and you leave it all to your spouse, when your spouse dies he will have too large of an estate to pass tax-free.

EXAMPLE:

> Marcy Brown has assets of $2,000,000. Her husband Jeff Brown has no assets. Marcy and Jeff have three children, Robert, Judd, and Heathcliff. Marcy dies, and her will leaves everything to Jeff. No estate tax is due because Marcy's estate used her unlimited marital deduction. Jeff dies shortly thereafter. Jeff's will states that his estate goes to his wife Marcy, if living, otherwise to Robert, Judd, and Heathcliff. Jeff's estate, now consisting of $2,000,000 that he received from Marcy, will pass to the three children. Only $1,000,000 is exempt, so estate taxes will be charged against the $1,000,000 difference.

Estate taxes can also sneak up unsuspectingly when you use the most common method of informal estate planning: the joint tenancy. Joint tenancy, as we saw earlier, passes assets automatically to the survivor. Joint tenancies between spouses also use the unlimited marital deduction, lumping assets all in the estate of the surviving spouse. This is probably the most common scenario of all.

EXAMPLE:

> Marcy and Jeff have a $2,000,000 estate, but it is all held in joint tenancy between themselves. When Marcy dies, Jeff does not have to worry about estate taxes, as the joint tenancies are covered by the unlimited marital deduction. As in our previous example, when Jeff dies, Robert, Judd, and Heathcliff will have their inheritance reduced by the estate taxes levied on the $1,000,000 excess.

How bad is the estate tax? It is one of the steepest taxes the federal government ever placed on the books. It is a graduated rate that increases as the amount subject to the tax gets larger. The rate can be over 40%. It can be a staggering sum to pay and is usually owed in less than a year after death.

All previous examples in this chapter have assumed the value of the estate. To understand how the government applies the basic estate and gift tax rule, we need to know to what estate it applies. In other words, what assets are subject to estate tax? The answer is any asset in which a decedent had an interest when he died. In other words, all bank accounts, mutual funds, stocks, bonds, real estate, etc. which is titled at least partially in your name or which is held in joint tenancy with someone else makes up your estate. The one type of asset most often overlooked in calculating the size of an estate is life insurance. If you have any ownership rights to an insurance policy on your life, the death benefit is included in your estate. An ownership right includes the right to cancel the policy, assign it, borrow against it, or even change the beneficiary. When in doubt, assume you own the policy—most people do have ownership rights—and assume that the death benefit is added to your estate. This can inflate the value of your estate rapidly.

EXAMPLE:

> Jesse James rents an apartment. He has about $500,000 in various bank accounts and investments. He has $100,000 in his company 401(k) retirement plan. He has a life insurance policy with a $300,000 death benefit with Prudopolitan Life, and his company provides an insurance policy as a company benefit to him which would pay $250,000 if he died. He also has a large gun collection valued at about $50,000. Jesse's estate would be valued at $1,200,000.

If you calculate the value of your estate and you arrive at a total over the exemption equivalent, you may wish to look at tax planning as another component in protecting your assets upon death. With proper planning, each spouse of a married couple can use his or her exemption amount. Assuming our $1,000,000 exemption amount this results in $2,000,000 passing tax-free to beneficiaries. The most common way to utilize both spouses' exemption is using our old friend, the trust. Let's look at two examples to see how couples, using a trust, can plan effectively for estate tax savings.

EXAMPLE:

> Phil and Laura have two children: Ryan and Erin. They have an estate of $2,000,000. To avoid estate tax, Phil and Laura split their assets so each has $1,000,000 titled in his or her respective name. Then Phil and Laura each sign wills. Each will says that all assets go directly to their two children. They think about their plan. They assume that Phil dies first. His will leaves $1,000,000 to Ryan and Erin. There is no estate tax owed, because Phil could leave that amount tax-free. They next assume that Laura would die soon after Phil. Her will leaves her $1,000,000 to the children, resulting in no estate tax on her estate either.

Phil and Laura may have avoided estate tax, but their plan has a glaring flaw. The plan deprives the surviving spouse of one-half of the family assets, with which he or she may need to live. They seek advice from an estate-planning attorney who suggests an alternative plan.

EXAMPLE:

After meeting with Michael, their attorney, Phil and Laura create two revocable declarations of trust. They split their assets, placing $1,000,000 into each trust. They re-examine their plan and discover that, if Phil died first, his trust splits into two sub-trusts: a family trust and a marital trust. The family sub-trust will hold an amount equal to Phil's exemption equivalent—$1,000,000 by today's laws—and the marital sub-trust will hold anything Phil's estate has in excess of that amount. Because Phil's declaration of trust currently has $1,000,000 worth of assets in it, Phil and Laura understand that a marital sub-trust would not be created, but that all assets would be held under the family sub-trust. The terms of the family sub-trust allow Laura, acting as a co-trustee together with another family member, to distribute all the income from the family trust to her. Laura would also be entitled to use principal from the family trust (in other words, dip into the assets themselves) if she needed it to maintain her standard of living and if the co-trustee approved. If Laura should die, the family trust distributes to the two children. The family sub-trust, when structured this way, uses Phil's exemption equivalent, and his estate is not taxed. When Laura later dies, her trust holds the remaining $1,000,000 of their assets and would pass estate tax free also, using her exemption equivalent.

This plan makes Phil and Laura more comfortable. It allows a surviving spouse access to funds held within the trust of the first spouse to die. It allows them to use both of their exemption equivalents, passing $2,000,000 estate tax free to children. It has "two strings" on the funds available for the surviving spouse in the deceased spouse's trust. First, some conservative attorneys believe that there must be a co-trustee together with the surviving spouse to manage the trust. Second, there must be a restriction on principal coming out of that trust. With those two strings in place, the trust will qualify for the estate tax exemption.

What if Phil's trust held more than $1,000,000? The amount in excess of the exemption equivalent goes into a marital sub-trust. Usually, a marital sub-trust allows a spouse unlimited access to the funds. If a couple has children from prior marriages, restrictions can be placed on the funds in the marital sub-trust as well. (This is discussed more fully in our next chapter.) In either case, the marital sub-trust qualifies for the unlimited marital deduction. The net effect is that Phil's estate, whether $1,000,000 or more, uses his full exemption equivalent, and will use the unlimited marital as needed to avoid estate taxation completely on his death.

The examples above both assumed Phil died first. Laura's estate plan would probably be a direct mirror image of Phil's. It would make no difference, then, if Laura died first.

This plan is basic "estate planning 101" for married couples with estates over the exemption amount. What about singles with larger estates? Or married couples with very large estates? Plans exist for persons in these categories. One we have already discussed: annual gifts of $12,000. Other plans besides gifting are possible. Here, however, we venture outside the area of basic planning, and into "estate planning 201," which is outside the scope of this book.

What is within the scope of this book is the understanding that an estate in excess of the federal exemption equivalent should cause you to seek professional advice, whether you are single or married. In addition, remember that the exemption equivalent is changing, but unless the law is amended again, will return to $1,000,000 in 2011. If you understand the dollar amount at which planning becomes a must, the basic rule of the exemption equivalent, and its two exceptions, the unlimited marital deduction and the annual exclusion, you understand the fundamentals of the federal estate and gift tax system. With fundamentals in hand you can evaluate if you need an estate tax plan to protect your assets. If you do choose to evaluate your options, know that this is a highly technical area, made simple for purposes of this basic discussion. In addition, some states have estate or inheritance tax considerations that affect larger estates. These additional state specific rules impact planning. If you have a potentially taxable estate, seek help from a qualified professional. Estate tax planning is not an area for the do-it-yourselfer!

10

It's a Family Affair: Problems with Beneficiaries and How to Plan to Avoid Them

In previous chapters we looked at how to protect your estate from various concerns that arise upon death. Many of us want our children and loved ones to inherit from us with a minimum of complication and inconvenience. Avoiding probate through the use of a living trust is one way to plan so that your estate is easier to settle. We also looked at how gift and estate taxation can shrink your estate and the planning options that exist to avoid these taxes. Finally, we considered minor beneficiaries, estate contests, and issues of privacy: legitimate concerns we all have.

This chapter focuses on concerns you might have about the beneficiaries of your estate. Suppose you die and your son is going to receive an inheritance from you. What if he is in the middle of a bitter and messy divorce? What if he is being sued in a multimillion-dollar lawsuit? Imagine that he has a great many unpaid bills and creditors at his heels. Does the inheritance you worked a lifetime to save immediately wind up in everyone's pockets but your son's?

What if you remarry? Second marriages are increasingly popular. It is not only the young that divorce and remarry, but older adults also wed after divorce or the death of a spouse. Suppose you are widowed and remarry. Your second spouse has adult children as do you. How do you make sure that your estate will eventually wind up in your children's hands and not the hands of the children of your spouse? Your spouse may want the same for her family as well.

Many families have one problem child: the "black sheep" of the brood. If you have such a person in your family, you may want to leave him less (or even none) of your estate. But how do you protect against the black sheep contesting your estate and costing the rest of the family time and money fighting him off?

These three issues all focus on the beneficiaries of your estate. Will you have a beneficiary in trouble: divorcing, in debt or defending a suit? Will your primary beneficiary—your spouse—be in a position to take care of your children from a previous marriage when he or she dies? Will the contemptuous child—the "black sheep"—be able to successfully contest your estate plan and tie up the interests of your other beneficiaries in the court system?

Let's look at the black sheep problem first. Misconceptions abound about how to disinherit the black sheep while trying to avoid his challenges to an estate such as a will contest.

EXAMPLE:

Adam, an aging widower, has a modest estate. His assets consist of some bank accounts and miscellaneous personal effects. The total value of his estate is about $50,000. Adam has two sons, Cain and Abel. Abel has been a good son to Adam. He is his father's pride and joy and he has done all he could throughout the years to be a devoted child. Cain, a rebellious youth, never grew up. He spends his time in pool halls and taverns, smoking, drinking, and running around. He has little use for his father, as his father cannot afford to let him mooch. Adam visits his local lawyer, Gordon Idol, and tells Gordon that he wants a will where Abel gets it all. He asks Gordon if he should "leave Cain a dollar," as Adam has heard that he should put a one dollar bequest in a will to fend off any challenges Cain might make.

Leaving a natural heir of an estate "one dollar" or some other nominal sum will probably do nothing but enrage him. A small bequest does little to prevent challenges to a will or trust. It does acknowledge that the creator of the will was aware of whom his family was, but that can be done just as easily by reciting their names in the will.

EXAMPLE:

> Adam has two choices on how to word the Second Article to his will: "Second: I leave one dollar to my son, Cain, and all residue of my estate to my son, Abel." Or: "Second: I have two children: Cain and Abel. I leave all residue of my estate to my son, Abel."

Which of the two examples above is most effective in preventing Cain from mounting a will contest? Legally, there is not much difference. Both correctly identify Adam's closest kin. Both are equally ineffective to guard his estate for Cain.

A better method to guard against estate contests is to leave a more significant sum of money to a black sheep, but have your will also contain a clause that provides that anyone who challenges the will forfeits his or her inheritance. This type of provision is known by a Latin phrase: the *in terrorem* clause. The *in terrorem* clause describes the job it is to do: to strike terror in the heart of one who would challenge a will or trust. This provision, when coupled with a more significant bequest, provides better protection against contests.

EXAMPLE:

> After consulting with Gordon Idol, Adam's will leaves the lesser of 10% of his estate or $5,000 to Cain, and the balance to Abel. Adam's will also contains an additional article, which reads: "I intentionally have provided for differing shares to be distributed to my children, or to a deceased child's descendants, if a child predeceases me. If any person who is given any interest in my will commences or joins (except as a defendant) any proceeding to contest the validity of this will or any of its provisions, all benefits provided to that person under this will are revoked, and those benefits shall pass as if that person died before me, leaving no descendants."

What did Gordon Idol, Adam's clever lawyer, accomplish by suggesting that Adam leave some money to Cain while putting the *in terrorem* clause in the will? Recall that in Chapter 8, we looked at how a will contest is easy to file, but tough to prove. However, if a person has something to lose by merely filing suit, he may think twice. Cain, as disgruntled as he may be, will think twice about filing suit to contest the will because the likely result is he will lose all his inheritance, plus owe a lawyer some fees.

In terrorem clauses can be placed in trusts as well. Remember in Chapter 8 we discussed how a trust was harder to contest than a will. If Adam had a $300,000 estate rather than $50,000, he might have opted to create a trust, with a small bequest to Cain and an *in terrorem* clause in the trust. That would afford, perhaps, the best protection against an estate contest that can be put into a document.

In terrorem clauses vary in complexity. The example noted above is fairly simple. *In terrorem* clauses can be written to cover a multitude of conditions. Many lawyers prefer a "kitchen sink" approach and place very lengthy and thorough clauses in wills and trusts.

The *in terrorem* clause, while good protection, is not 100% foolproof. *In terrorem* clauses have been challenged in court by persistent black sheep and overturned. Thus, if you have a black sheep, the delicate balance to strike is the amount of the bequest that you think will discourage him from even filing suit.

EXAMPLE:

> John has a $400,000 estate and three sons, George, Paul and Ringo. Ringo is the "black sheep" in John's family. If John leaves 1/3 to each son, Ringo would have almost no incentive to contest John's estate. If John leaves ½ each to Paul and George, and nothing to the black sheep, Ringo will go straight from the funeral home to his lawyer's office, retainer money in hand. Obviously, the closer that Ringo's share under John's estate gets to 1/3, the less likely it is that he will file a contest. But how much is enough? Will a $5,000 bequest do it? How about 10% of the estate? 20%? John is the right person to come up with the best guess. John needs to convey his guess to his attorney, Abbey Rhodes, so that Abbey can prepare a plan to meet his particular family situation. Unfortunately, this is not an exact science!

Suppose that instead of being a black sheep, Ringo is a well meaning child, but one who is embroiled in complex litigation. In our earlier example, what if Cain is not smoking, drinking, and running around, but his wife is, and she is running up the credit card bills to do it. Presume instead that Cain or Ringo are not black sheep, but that each married a shrew that he has failed to tame. Entanglements with creditors, soon to be ex-wives or lawsuits, imperil the inheritance each might receive.

A trust that you create and fund with your assets can protect these assets from creditors or ex-spouses of your beneficiaries, or judgments from lawsuits against them. Another clause can be placed into a trust that will protect trust assets from creditors, failed marriages and more. This provision is called a spendthrift clause. It permits a beneficiary to voluntarily withdraw funds from a trust, but restricts someone from compelling a beneficiary to do so.

To draft an effective spendthrift clause into the document, your trust must not mandate that the trustee distribute the trust after the bills of your estate have been paid. Instead, the trust must continue for a period—either until children or beneficiaries reach a certain age, until a set number of years after your death or until a child requests his or her inheritance—and allow a trustee to manage the funds held for the beneficiaries' welfare. This does not mean the inheritance of a child or beneficiary is locked away. A trust can allow a beneficiary to voluntarily withdraw any or all his share. The trust's spendthrift clause prohibits attachment by creditors or ex-spouses.

EXAMPLE:

> Shaquille is a wealthy retired businessman. He is widowed, with one son, Jordan. Shaquille loves his son dearly, but does not approve of Jordan's wife. He is concerned that Jordan may someday divorce his troublesome spouse. Shaquille creates a trust that leaves his entire estate to Jordan. Bull National Bank is the trustee of the trust after Shaquille dies. Although the trust leaves everything to Jordan when Shaquille dies, it also retains the inheritance in trust. The trust further states: "my child may withdraw any part or all the principal of his share at any time or times. The trustee of my trust pays the requested amount upon the child's written, voluntary request. The trustee shall not allow an involuntary exercise of this withdrawal power. The interests of my child in his share, whether in principal or income, shall not be subject to the claims of any creditor, any spouse for alimony or support, or others, or to legal process, and may not be voluntarily or involuntarily transferred or encumbered."

This language creates a spendthrift trust for Jordan's inheritance. It allows Jordan to take any or all his inheritance if the seas are calm. But if Jordan is encountering stormy seas, such as a divorce or other litigation, or creditor problems, Jordan can elect to leave his inheritance in trust. A creditor or spouse should not be able to force Jordan to pull his inheritance from the trust so that it can be used to satisfy those obligations.

The spendthrift trust does not lock away the funds from beneficiary's use even if problems are occurring. Additional language is placed into these trusts that allows the trustee to pay income and principal to or for the benefit of the beneficiary in the trustee's discretion. You can also give guidance to the trustee. The trust can direct the trustee to spend income or principal on health, maintenance, education, or other needs of the beneficiary. The important language is the restriction on forcing a beneficiary to withdraw funds.

In the example we looked at, Shaquille named a bank as successor trustee in his trust. What if Shaquille wanted his son Jordan to be successor trustee? Can he do that and still retain the spendthrift provisions if needed?

If the beneficiary and trustee is the same person, you cannot have an effective spendthrift provision. You can, however, provide for a second successor trustee that will take over if your first choice resigns. In that case, the spendthrift clause should be effective.

EXAMPLE:

> Shaquille named Jordan as the successor trustee of his trust, and Bull National Bank as second successor trustee. Shaquille dies. Jordan is undergoing a messy divorce, so he declines to act as successor trustee. Bull National Bank will then act as trustee. The spendthrift clause should be effective to protect Jordan's inheritance from his soon-to-be ex-wife.

Although a will can contain trust provisions with a spendthrift clause, the living trust is the better, more comprehensive approach. You are able to combine the asset protection of a spendthrift clause with the other advantages of a living trust.

You may wonder if a spendthrift clause can protect your assets from your creditors during your lifetime. Could you create a trust agreement with a bank or other third party and put spendthrift clauses to protect assets while you are alive?

There is a myth afoot that living trusts protect assets from its creator's creditors. The basic rule in most of the countries that recognize trusts is that you cannot create a self-settled spendthrift trust: a spendthrift trust into which you place your own assets. This is also true in nearly every state in our country. The prohibition against self-settled spendthrift trusts is an ancient one, dating back 400 years. In the late 1500s, the English passed a law, known as the Statute of Elizabeth, which effectively prohibits self-settled spendthrift trusts. It states that if you create a trust with your own assets, and your trust gives the trustee any discretion to pay income or principal back to you, then the trust is vulnerable to your creditors.

EXAMPLE:

> Donald creates a trust with Tower Bank as trustee. He places his assets into the trust. The trust gives Tower sole and absolute discretion, to pay or to refuse to pay, income or principal to Donald. Donald is hit by double trouble: His wife, Ivana, is divorcing him, and several real estate deals he entered into are failing. He is being pursued by Ivana's lawyers and is being sued by his partners in the real estate deals. The lawyers for both serve Tower Bank with a court order to turn over assets to satisfy judgments against Donald. Under the Statute of Elizabeth (and modern laws that restate it) Tower must comply. Donald's attempt to shelter assets fails.

In general, if you have any interest in a trust, it is available to satisfy creditors, judgments and ex-spouses. Assets can be safe only if you give up all interest.

EXAMPLE:

> Donald creates a trust agreement with Tower Bank. The trust pays income to Donald's children, and then distributes the principal to the children when they reach age 25. Donald can never receive principal or income from the trust. Several years later, Ivana sues Donald for divorce, and his partners sue him for some bad business dealings. His trust agreement should be safe.

Most persons do not want to give up complete control over their assets in order to protect them. Thus, a self-settled trust is generally not an effective asset protection tool.

A few states have overruled the Statute of Elizabeth. Both Alaska and Delaware recently passed some amendments to their trust laws allowing self-settled spendthrift trusts. At first glance this may seem attractive. Why not create a trust agreement with a bank in Alaska or Delaware, allowing the trustee to use its discretion to pay income and principal to you?

You have three things to think about if you consider an Alaskan or similar spendthrift trust. First, the Alaskan statute that allows these trusts passed in spring of 1997. (Delaware followed later.) Thus, the concept is untested in the courts as no one has, to date, attempted to reach assets in an Alaskan trust. We do not know how the courts will view these trusts. Second, Alaska (and Delaware) cannot override federal laws. If you are declaring bankruptcy, or have litigation ongoing because of some violation of a federal law, or are in trouble with the IRS, and have assets in an Alaska-based trust, a federal court will likely override the state of Alaska's trust laws, and find the trust assets available to pay for these problems. Finally, the trust must still be discretionary. You cannot have the absolute right to revoke the trust or compel the trustee to distribute assets from the trust back to you. If you did, then a court would simply order you to withdraw assets to satisfy a creditor or judgment.

You can create a self-settled spendthrift trust that will eliminate some of the problems with the Alaskan or Delaware trusts if you broaden your horizons. Countries other than the U.S. have enacted laws similar to these two states that permit these types of trusts. Unlike Alaska or Delaware, however, these trusts have a longer track record and we are more certain how courts will view them. These trusts may also protect against some federal laws; for example, a foreign spendthrift trust may insulate assets in bankruptcy court. You cannot insulate assets from the IRS. We will examine these trusts in more detail in Chapter 15.

One thing you cannot do with a self-settled spendthrift trust, whether based in Alaska, Delaware, or another country, is frustrate current or potential creditors. If you know of creditors or impending action, you cannot take steps to create these trusts. This violates what are known as "fraudulent conveyancing laws." You cannot attempt to defraud a current or known creditor. There is more about this caution in Chapter 15 as well.

A final problem arises when persons remarry, with children from previous marriages. Most commonly, a person in that situation wants an estate plan that provides first for her spouse, but if her spouse predeceases her, she wants to provide for her children, and not her spouse's children. Probably the most common estate plan in America is a will coupled with jointly owned assets. This can be a disaster in second marriage situations.

EXAMPLE:

> Anne has one son: Brett. She marries Michael, who also has one child, his daughter Marilee. Michael and Anne put all their assets into joint tenancy. Michael has a will stating that all assets go to Anne, if living, otherwise to his daughter. Anne's will leaves all to Michael, if living, otherwise to her son. Michael dies. Anne now has control of all the family assets due to the joint tenancies. Anne then dies shortly thereafter, and her will leaves all the family assets to Brett. Marilee is not pleased.

One way to correct his situation is to use our old friend, the living trust.

EXAMPLE:

> Instead of joint tenancies or a will Michael prepares a trust that makes his sister, Trixie, co-trustee with Anne when Michael dies. The trust provides for Anne during her lifetime. The trust further states that when Anne dies, the trust distributes to Marilee. Anne does a similar trust, but her ultimate beneficiary when both she and Michael are deceased is her son. Michael and Anne title the assets they brought into the marriage into their respective trusts. By agreement, they split assets they acquire during their marriage into one trust or the other. The trusts can meet the two goals of providing for a spouse while ensuring that children are not disinherited.

One key to ensuring that a trust can prevent disinheritance is to have a third party act as trustee. In our example, Michael used his sister to act as co-trustee with Anne. This provides a check against Anne simply appropriating all the trust assets to the ultimate detriment of Michael's daughter. In your situation, consider if a family member is a good choice. A bank or trust company may be a better alternative to an unwilling or inappropriate family member.

While outside of the scope of this book, second marriages with pre-existing children need more than trusts to create an effective estate plan. A pre-marital agreement is a necessity. Pre-marital agreements generally cover two situations: divorce and death. These agreements can spell out details required to be in estate plans, present and contemplated, and can help prevent challenges to trusts, ensuring a successful estate plan.

Second marriages, black sheep, and the problems with your beneficiaries' creditors or ex-spouses are challenges to the estate plan. You need to account for all three if you want the assets protected in your estate at death. Lifetime protection of assets is the goal of our next and final section of this book. Instead of focusing in general on creditors or lawsuits, however, we will focus on the greatest threat to a lifetime of savings and hard work: the need for long-term care in a nursing home.

11

The Residence of Last Resort: The Decision to Enter a Nursing Home

If you walk into any local nursing home and take a poll, you will not find too many residents who delight in being there. Many may have accepted that they have no other alternative. Others still want to go home, wherever home may be. If given a choice, none of us chooses a nursing home as our first choice of residence.

Unfortunately, illness and infirmity robs us of choice. There may come a time when you, your spouse, or your parent can no longer live at home in the community. Home care or assisted living may have already been tried and found wanting. The nursing home may become the only alternative left.

Sometimes, the nursing home is a forced alternative. If you are single, or have a spouse who cannot care for you, you may not have the family support necessary to remain in your home. You may not have the money to pay for other alternatives such as live-in companions or senior communities that are less restrictive than a nursing home. As we will see in our next chapter, there are government programs that provide financial aid to the disabled elderly. But these programs are geared toward residency in nursing homes. Little government help is available to those who reside in the community, but need assistance in dressing, eating, mobility, toileting or other activities of daily living. You find that the government programs tacitly encourage your move to a nursing facility.

Nursing homes are expensive places to live. Long-term care is one of the greatest threats to your assets and your estate. The final section of this book deals with that threat. Even a short stay in a nursing home can wipe out a lifetime of savings. In addition to planning for asset protection in the event of incompetency and death, you may need a plan to preserve assets from depletion due to long-term healthcare needs.

Prior to heading into the asset protection side of long-term healthcare, however, this chapter will examine some other issues that crop up any time nursing home admission is imminent. If you or your spouse or parent needs a nursing home, you must make a wise choice. From a financial standpoint, the choice of nursing home can be the single largest financial decision you make in your life. It can easily eclipse buying a car, a home or even a business. Finances aside, you need to be sure that the facility provides the best care possible. Living in a sub-par nursing home to save a few bucks is not a good trade-off for anyone!

This chapter will look at some tools to help you pick the best facility for yourself, your husband, your wife or your parent. Comparing two or more nursing homes is difficult. This chapter contains some lists of concrete things to look for in a nursing home. You can look at facilities objectively without having to rely upon "gut feelings."

We will also look at some of the nitty gritty details that contracts for admission to nursing homes contain. Many of us go over contracts to buy a car with care. We often hire lawyers to prepare or review an agreement to purchase a home. Yet too often, a person will sign a contract to admit a family member to a nursing home without even reading the entire document. This chapter will alert you to some common provisions to avoid in an admissions contract.

Before you even sign a contract, however, you need to tour several nursing homes. Try to visit at least three, if time permits. Unfortunately, if the person for whom you are seeking admission is in the hospital, you may get only a days' notice prior to discharge. A 24-hour whirlwind tour of nursing homes is not the best scenario. It may be the scenario forced upon you.

When you tour area nursing homes, take a pad of paper or notebook and pen. Spend time in each facility and take extensive notes. Consider the following concerns when you visit each nursing home:

1. Where is the nursing home? Is it close to family and friends that will visit the person who will reside there?

2. Is the home clean and neat? Is it an attractive place to live? Does it smell bad? Does it smell like urine or other unpleasant odors?

3. Is the nursing home well lit? Is it cheerful and bright or dark and depressing? Is the temperature reasonable?

4. Are all areas of the home handicapped accessible? Are wheelchair ramps present? Do the hallways and rooms have handrails or other grab bars for safety?

5. Are there smoke detectors, sprinkler systems, and/or fire alarms? What is the plan to evacuate the home if a fire strikes? Are there fire extinguishers?

6. Are exits clearly marked and unobstructed?

7. Is smoking allowed in the nursing home? If so, is it restricted to certain areas or to patient's rooms who smoke?

8. What outside dental and medical services are available? What ambulance service is used? How far is the nursing home from the nearest hospital or trauma center?

9. How are drugs obtained—from an in-house pharmacy or contracted with an outside agency? When drugs are on the premises, are they kept in a secure, locked area away from residents? Who monitors the resident's medications?

10. Is at least one registered nurse or licensed practical nurse on duty 24 hours a day? Does a registered nurse serve as Director of Nursing Services?

11. Are there emergency call buttons by each resident's bed and in every washroom?

12. Are physical therapy, speech therapy, and occupational therapy services offered on-site? Does the nursing home have a high number of residents who engage in various types of therapy?

13. What kinds of social services and activities does the home have? Can family members participate? What space is used for social services?

14. For those residents who are able, are trips outside the nursing home available? Is there an outside patio area or something similar so that residents can go outside on pleasant days?

15. Are religious services offered on site? For what denominations?

16. Does each resident's room have a window and adequate light and ventilation? Are there private spaces or screening in each room? Are there separate conference rooms where a resident could meet privately with family, a lawyer, or clergy?

17. Are private telephones available in the room? What is the cost? Is there a public phone?

18. What are the visiting hours? Is there a place at the front where visitors sign in and out? What kind of security exists?

19. Examine the kitchen. Is it clean? Is food properly stored or is there food standing on counters?

20. Ask to have a meal at the nursing home. Is the food reasonably appetizing and well prepared?

21. What types of special meals are available? When are meals served? Can a resident get between meal snacks?

22. Will the nursing home offer names of families who would give references to you? If not (and privacy may not permit), introduce yourself

to family members visiting other residents and ask opinions about the facility.

23. Are the home and its administrator licensed? Have there been any licensing suspensions or other problems recently?

24. Do residents look well cared for, appropriately groomed and dressed? Does the staff seem attentive to residents?

25. Is there a written statement of resident's rights? Ask to be provided a copy.

26. Does the facility participate in the Medicare program?

27. Does the facility participate in the Medicaid program?

28. What forms does the facility ask you to fill out prior to admission? Ask to obtain blank copies of the forms so that you can take them home and read them over.

29. Ask specifically for a blank copy of the admissions contract. You want to take that home and study it with care.

If after your tours you have narrowed down your choices, you should next turn to the sample contract you picked up from the nursing home you feel is the best. You may consider having an attorney review the contract with you. There are several things to look for in any nursing home contract. Consider the following:

1. Are the terms of the contract clear? Does it spell out exactly the basic room rate? Does it have a section of optional services and additional charges? Do you feel you can estimate the monthly cost of care accurately from a plain reading of the contract? Does it seem that some services are omitted from the contract?

2. How big is the typeface? Is the type so small that you or the nursing home resident may have difficulty reading it?

3. Does the nursing home require that a "responsible party" other than the resident sign the contract? Do they insist on this even though the resident is competent to enter into the contract by himself?

4. Does the contract state that the "responsible party" is a "guarantor" of payment? While guarantor provisions under federal law become void if the resident obtains Medicaid, should problems arise securing eligibility, another family member's assets could be tapped to pay the bills.

5. Is there blanket consent to all types of medical treatment? Does it require the resident to choose a particular physician? Both of these provisions are offensive and may be illegal in your state.

6. Is there a clause where you are asked to guarantee a certain length of stay? These clauses can be illegal as well.

7. Does the contract ask in writing, or has an admissions person asked orally, for a "contribution" prior to obtaining Medicaid coverage for a resident? This practice, once common, is illegal.

8. Does the contract clearly state the reasons a resident can be discharged? Generally, a resident can only be discharged for non-payment, or for the welfare of the resident or of other residents. Awaiting a decision on a Medicaid application is not to be considered non-payment.

9. Be aware that no matter how it is termed, the admissions agreement is a contract that is legally binding. It may obligate you and your family to paying more money to the nursing home than you paid for your house!

10. You should strongly consider hiring a knowledgeable attorney to review the contract before you sign it.

If you have an agreeable contract with a facility that you feel provides good care, you can now look to the asset protection side of the nursing home decision. Before we leave the decision to pick a nursing home behind, you need to be aware that honesty with the nursing home is important. As we will learn in subsequent chapters, you may be able to obtain government assistance to pay for the nursing home. This assistance is key in preserving and protecting your assets. Obtaining this assistance is done in full disclosure to the nursing home as well as to the government agencies that screen applications for assistance. Nothing we will discuss in the following chapters relies upon secrecy or misrepresentation. The nursing home is your partner in care for a loved one. Even if you could, why try to "put one over" on the facility that is watching over your spouse or parent?

12

Uncle Sam Lends a Hand: Understanding Medicare and Medicaid Assistance with Nursing Home Costs

Perhaps nothing is more devastating to your estate than enormous nursing home bills. With the cost of private pay in a nursing home averaging between $4,000 and $9,000 or more per month, rapid depletion of virtually every modest estate is assured when a person needs long-term care. Medicare is the single largest payer of basic healthcare costs for seniors. Medicare and Medicare supplemental insurance policies, however, provide little in the way of benefits for long-term healthcare needs.

If you or your spouse need care in a nursing home, without Medicare and Medicare supplemental insurance providing any significant coverage you are left with three possible ways to pay: private pay (that is, out of your income and assets), long-term care insurance that you had previously purchased, or Medicaid.

Long-term care insurance currently pays less than 5% of the total cost of nursing home stays. Very few individuals have purchased this type of insurance. If you already have some health problems, you may no longer be eligible to buy this kind of policy, or if you do pass underwriting, your benefits will be limited or excluded if your nursing home stay results from your current health problem. Long-term care insurance can also be quite pricey. With long-term care insurance paying for only a small percentage of nursing home stays, the burden falls upon private pay sources and Medicaid. If you were to total the cost of all nursing home stays in America, you would find that Medicaid and private pay each account for about 45% of the payments for long-term care.

Medicaid, like Medicare, is a government program. Unlike Medicare, it includes payment for long-term nursing home care for those who qualify. Persons frequently confuse Medicaid and Medicare. The simplest way to understand the differences between the two is to remember simple one-word definitions for each: Medicare is insurance; Medicaid is welfare.

Medicare, as an insurance program, is available to all who reach age 65 and who are eligible for Social Security retirement benefits or railroad retirement benefits. Medicare is wholly federally funded and administered. As we noted above, Medicare pays for very little in the way of nursing home costs. It will only pay for short term-rehabilitation stays.

EXAMPLE:

> Martha Stewer, age 76, falls and breaks her hip while attempting to redecorate her home. She undergoes successful hip replacement surgery at the hospital. After a short recuperation in the hospital, her doctor recommends a six-week rehabilitation stay in a local Medicare-certified nursing home. Medicare will pay a portion of the costs of the stay.

While Medicare is not a solution for long-term care, it does provide some coverage for a common nursing home visit: the short-term recuperative or rehabilitative stay. Medicare will pay a portion of up to 100 days in a skilled nursing facility. It pays up to 20 days in full, and an additional 80 days subject to a copayment. The copayment is paid out of your pocket, unless you have a Medicare supplemental insurance. Frequently, Medicare supplemental insurance policies will cover some or all the copayment. You can also get an additional 100 days of coverage if a period of 60 days elapses since Medicare paid for previous skilled care.

Medicare coverage requires that you enter the nursing home following a hospital stay. The coverage is only for skilled care. Unfortunately, most long-term residents enter the nursing home without having been in a hospital first, and most require custodial or intermediate care. This is why Medicare is not helpful to a majority of long-term care residents. For some, however, Medicare will provide coverage, and should not be overlooked as a source of funds.

EXAMPLE:

> Willy Cosby is a nursing home resident receiving skilled care. Medicare is paying the bills. He remains in the nursing home after Medicare runs out, obtaining custodial care paid for out of his own funds. He breaks his hip three months later and enters the hospital, staying there for two weeks. When he returns to the nursing home, he needs rehabilitation and skilled care again. He may establish additional Medicare coverage.

For nursing home care to be covered by Medicare, four requirements must be met:

1. the care received must be skilled care given on a daily basis;

2. it must be care that can be given only in a skilled nursing facility on an in-patient basis;

3. the nursing home must be a Medicare-certified facility; and

4. the person must enter the home after a hospitalization stay of three days or more.

The most common denials of Medicare coverage are based on the requirement that skilled care be provided. The federal statutes and regulations that govern the Medicare system define skilled care as that which is so inherently complex that it can be safely and effectively performed only by or under the supervision of professional or technical personnel such as registered nurses, licensed practical nurses, physical therapists, occupational therapists, and speech pathologists. The regulations further list five specific types of skilled care:

1. care that is developed, managed and evaluated based on physician's orders as part of the overall management and evaluation of a care plan

2. skilled care necessary for the observation and assessment of a patient's condition, required to identify and evaluate the patient's need for modification of treatment or additional medical procedures

3. patient educational services needed to teach a patient self-maintenance

4. skilled nursing services—examples include:

    a. intravenous injections or feedings

    b. nasogastric or other tube feedings

    c. dressings applied with medications or other specific medical techniques

    d. treatment of extensive bed sores

    e. insertion or replacement of catheters

5. skilled rehabilitation, performed by licensed therapists

Coverage is frequently denied for Medicare coverage based on in-house assessments performed within the skilled nursing facilities. If you are denied coverage, you have the right to appeal this denial. You would first request a "demand submission." This is a claim submitted by the nursing facility to the "fiscal intermediary." The fiscal intermediary is a private insurance company that contracts with Medicare to process claims. The fiscal intermediary will provide you with an "initial determination." This may be the first official Medicare denial of the claim. You may then file a request for reconsideration with the fiscal intermediary. If there is $100 or more in controversy, a further appeal of a denial of the reconsideration request may be made to an Administrative Law Judge. An appeal of the decision of an Administrative Law Judge may be made to the Social Security Appeals Council. If $1,000 or more is in controversy, the next steps will take you into federal district court.

Strict and limited time periods are allowed at each stage of the appeal process. If you want to appeal, you should be advised to seek competent advice from a professional versed in Medicare law.

As you can see, obtaining Medicare coverage in a nursing home setting is a complex and confusing process. You may feel overwhelmed by the rules of the Medicare system. However, your uneasiness with the Medicare rules should not hamper you in planning to protect assets in a long-term care situation because Medicare, with its limited coverage, is not your best solution for long-term care. It can offer some additional assistance in paying for initial admissions. Don't overlook it as a source in the event you are in a nursing home, have to enter a hospital, and then later re-enter the nursing facility.

Curiously, current federal laws seem to encourage skilled nursing facilities to refuse to submit Medicare claims. If a facility believes that you might obtain Medicare coverage and it turns out later that Medicare denies the claim, then under the rules the facility is stuck with no one to bill! Thus, when in doubt, a facility will err on the side of denying a claim. If you are denied Medicare coverage, you should not be shy about pursuing at least the initial stages of an appeal. It costs little to do so, and you have nothing to lose.

Unlike Medicare, Medicaid provides significant payments for long-term care in nursing homes. As we noted, Medicaid is welfare: a needs-based program. It is available only if you meet certain financial criteria. Medicaid is jointly funded by the federal government and each state. Each state administers its Medicaid program through a state public aid agency. The states are free to tailor Medicaid rules within federal guidelines. Thus, the Medicaid program varies considerably from state to state. You must consult the regulations in your state to determine the exact rules you might encounter. This chapter will provide you with an outline. The outline is generic and intended to provide basic information.

As a form of welfare Medicaid rules can and do change frequently. Planning for long-term care taking into account the Medicaid system carries with it a certain amount of risk. "Grandfathering" of an existing situation under which you may qualify for Medicaid when the rules change is uncertain. Extreme caution should be exercised.

To understand how you or your spouse or parent would gain Medicaid eligibility, it is first necessary to understand the Medicaid rules. For nursing home care, there are five sets of rules to examine: rules on liens, rules on estate claims, income rules, asset rules and transfer of asset rules.

Under certain circumstances, the state Medicaid agency can place a lien on the real estate owned by a Medicaid recipient or his or her spouse. A lien is a claim for payment of money, recorded against title to real estate. Liens make it difficult to sell property, as virtually no one will buy property that has a lien upon it. The Medicaid lien may be recorded any time after a person begins to receive Medicaid. However, it will not be enforced until the death of the Medicaid recipient or the sale of the property. The lien rules do not directly affect the eligibility of a nursing home resident to obtain Medicaid. Liens are one way in which the states attempt to collect repayment for Medicaid services provided after a Medicaid recipient or spouse dies. Enforcement of the lien rules seems to vary somewhat from state to state.

When a Medicaid recipient dies, the state agency has the right to file a claim against his or her estate. This claim, like a lien, is designed so that the state may receive reimbursement for any amounts paid on behalf of the recipient. Some state regulations provide for claims against probate estates, and are unclear as to the rights, if any, that the state has to pursue reimbursement against the recipients of non-probate assets such as joint tenancies or property passing under the terms of a living trust. The laws of other states allow the Medicaid agency to recover from non-probate assets.

The state also has the right to force a Medicaid recipient to renounce a will where his spouse has disinherited him, and claim a statutory share. In some states, a right to renounce an estate plan where a person has disinherited his spouse is limited to wills. No right of renunciation exists in these states against non-probatable estate plans: living trusts, joint tenancies or payable on death accounts. In addition, in most states, if the Medicaid recipient receives funds from a personal injury suit or settlement, the state agency usually has the right to collect payment from the personal injury recovery amounts the state has previously paid on behalf of the Medicaid recipient. This is known as a "charge" upon the recovery.

While the estate claim and lien rules do not affect your ability to obtain Medicaid coverage, they do affect your ability to leave an inheritance to your family. In forthcoming chapters, we will discuss ways to plan to protect inheritances from liens and claims. Without an awareness of the lien and estate claim rules, however, you fail to protect your assets from ultimate depletion due to long-term care needs. You can gain eligibility for Medicaid and your assets may be safe for you or your spouse's lifetime, but the state will simply collect its due when you die.

There are three sets of rules that determine initial eligibility for Medicaid: income rules, asset rules, and transfer of asset rules. We will first look at the two categories of income rules.

The first income rule involves income caps for eligibility. You need to check whether your state is an income cap state or not. For example, Indiana is not an income cap state, whereas Colorado has caps. In an income cap state, if you have too much income you can never qualify for Medicaid. Many caps are set much lower than the average private pay rate in nursing homes. Thus, income cap states can place you in a position where you are "too wealthy to qualify for Medicaid, yet too poor to afford private pay nursing care."

EXAMPLE:

Perry Como has spent several years in Las Vegas Nursing Center. Perry had some assets from a career in the music business, but his funds are now exhausted. Perry receives $1650 per month from social security and a musicians' union pension. Las Vegas Nursing Center charges $3,200 per month for Perry's care. The state Perry lives in is an income cap state. The cap is $1345 per month. Perry cannot qualify for Medicaid because his monthly income is over the cap. Perry's income falls far short of the private pay rate. He cannot afford to pay privately any more. He faces a difficult quandary.

In an income cap state, sometimes a reduction in income is desirable. The way some caps are set, social security plus a pension may bump you over the cap. There are ways to divert pension income to a spouse, which involves domestic relations court proceedings. Of course, competent legal advice is needed to pursue this option.

The second category of income rules apply if you have a spouse who is still healthy and living at home. A spouse at home, known in Medicaid jargon as the "community spouse," is allowed to keep a certain amount of income. The community spouse is generally allowed to keep all income that is payable in her name. This is sometimes referred to as the "name on the check" rule.

EXAMPLE:

Dorothy and her husband Oswald together receive $1550 per month. Oswald suffers from delusions that have left Dorothy with no choice but to admit him to Emerald Nursing Home. Oswald receives $700 social security per month. Dorothy receives $500 per month social security and a $350 monthly pension from her former job as a balloon pilot. Oswald has qualified for Medicaid to pay his nursing home bills. Dorothy can keep her $850 per month income because it is paid in her name.

Additionally, a community spouse is permitted to retain enough of the income of the institutionalized spouse to boost her income up to the "community spouse income allowance." The amount of the community spouse income allowance varies from state to state. Many states index the allowance yearly for inflation. For 2007 the maximum community spouse income allowance is $2,541 per month. The minimum is about one half of that amount.

EXAMPLE:

> Assume that in our previous example, Oswald received a monthly income of $2,000—$700 social security and $1300 pension from his career as a baker of poppy seed rolls. Assume that Dorothy's income is still $850 per month. The state Dorothy and Oswald live in has adopted the maximum community spouse income allowance. Not only can Dorothy keep her $850 per month, but $1691 from Oswald's income will be paid to Dorothy under the community spouse income allowance rule. This boosts her income to $2,541 per month. The remainder of Oswald's monthly income goes to pay his cost of care, for his Medicare supplement policy and towards a $30 per month personal needs allowance.

If the community spouse has income coming in her name that exceeds the income allowance rule, she can keep it all. She will not receive any of her spouse's income, however.

EXAMPLE:

> Suppose Dorothy Toto's income is $2,600 per month and Oswald's is $1,500. Dorothy will keep her $2,600, but will not receive any of Oswald's income.

Once you understand the two income rules, you can next look at perhaps the most important set of Medicaid rules: those dealing with assets. Assets are divided into two categories for Medicaid purposes: exempt assets and non-exempt assets. Exempt assets do not affect you or your spouse's eligibility for Medicaid. Non-exempt assets must be spent on private pay care or converted to exempt assets before you can qualify for Medicaid. Both spouses' assets are usually lumped together and considered as one for purposes of determining Medicaid eligibility.

The most important exempt asset is the family home. The home is not considered an asset available to be used for your care if your spouse lives there, if an adult disabled child or minor child lives there, or if you intend to return home after a nursing home stay. Proof of the intent to return home varies from state to state. The usual practice in many states is to require a doctor's statement that the intent to return home may be possible. If you leave your home with the intent to permanently reside in a nursing home and no other qualifying individual such as a spouse lives there, the home becomes non-exempt property. An additional rule added in February 2006, limits the equity in the family residence to no more than $500,000. States with higher value properties (California is probably the prime example) may allow a higher limit of up to $750,000.

Other exempt assets include personal items not exceeding $2,000 in value, life insurance or burial fund not exceeding $1,500 in face value, or a combination of the two, not exceeding $3,500 combined. Grave markers or burial spaces of unlimited value, including burial spaces for the recipient's spouse and other immediate family members are exempt. Wedding and engagement rings are exempt. One auto not exceeding $4,500 in value is exempt. Certain other items are exempt because of their protection under federal law. These items will probably never apply to your situation, but bear a brief mention. These items include: food stamp coupons; U.S. Department of Agriculture donated foods; supplemental food assistance under the Child Nutrition Program & National School Lunch Act; benefits received under the Nutrition Program for the Elderly or of the Older Americans Act of 1965; funds distributed to or held in trust for Indian tribes under certain public acts; payments received under Uniform Relocation Assistance and Real Property Acquisition Policies Act of 1970; tax-exempt portions of payments made under the Alaska Native Claims Settlement Act; Experimental Housing Allowance Program payments made under Annual Contributions Contracts under certain sections of the U.S.

Housing Act of 1937; receipts distributed to certain Indian tribunal members; payments to VISTA, SCOPE, and ACE volunteers; certain student loan funds; Supplement Security Income payments received by recipients who do not reside in certain group care facilities; certain state provided assistance to senior citizens for property tax relief or other needs; certain payments made by the U.S. government to citizens of Japanese ancestry who were interned during World War II; payments made to veterans from the Agent Orange Settlement Fund; and certain payments to Aleuts who were interned during World War II.

Another important category of exempt assets are those assets that are unavailable to you or your spouse. Examples of these include trusts that are irrevocable and allow none of the principal of the trust to be accessed for the benefit of the institutionalized person. Certain types of annuities and installment notes may also be unavailable assets. For a single Medicaid recipient, $2,000 in cash or other assets is also exempt.

If you are married, additional assets are exempt. The family residence will always be exempt (up to our limit of $500,000) if the spouse continues to reside there. Personal effects may be unlimited in value and still be exempt. One auto of unlimited value is exempt. Most importantly, a "community spouse resource allowance" is permitted as an exempt asset.

The community spouse resource allowance is made up of cash and other assets that the community spouse may retain without affecting the institutionalized spouse's Medicaid eligibility. The resource allowance may be tailored by each state within certain federal guidelines. The amount will change yearly based on the increase in inflation and the cost of living. For 2007, the maximum a state may use as a resource allowance is $101,640. Within a specified time period after approval by the state agency, usually about 90 days, the institutionalized spouse may transfer his assets to his community spouse in order to achieve the community spouse resource allowance.

EXAMPLE:

Bogie and Lauren Humphrey have the following assets between them: their family home, worth $100,000, a beach house in the Florida Keys, worth $50,000, and $29,000 in bank accounts. Bogie enters Casablanca Care Centre. The state in which the Humphreys reside adopted the maximum community spouse resource allowance. Lauren applies for Medicaid to pay Bogie's cost of care. Bogie is eligible immediately because all of the family assets are exempt: the house is exempt, and combined the cash and Florida property total $79,000, which Lauren can keep because it is less than the community spouse allowance. Bogie transfers his interest in the real property and the bank accounts to Lauren after he becomes eligible for Medicaid.

A transfer of assets between spouses is not only permitted under Medicatd laws, it is often mandatory to maintain a community spouse allowance. In some states, if the institutionalized spouse fails to transfer assets within a certain time period after eligibility is achieved, the community spouse allowance is forfeited.

Transfers of assets between spouses do not affect eligibility for Medicaid. However, many other transfers to persons other than spouses incur a penalty and a period of ineligibility for Medicaid. You could not give all your assets to your children, admit yourself to a nursing home, and ask Medicaid to pay the bill. Transfers like that violate our third set of Medicaid eligibility rules: the asset transfer rules.

Simply stated, a transfer of assets for less than fair market value will affect Medicaid eligibility. The transfer of assets rule is frequently the biggest "trap" for the unwary. The rule is intended to penalize gifting of assets, which is the primary means of transferring an asset for less than fair market value. Moreover, adding to the confusion, the rules on transfers of assets changed in February of 2006, affecting any transfers made after that date.

The basic rule for transfers **prior to February 2006**, is as follows:

> A transfer of assets for less than fair market value will disqualify the Medicaid applicant for the period for which the amount transferred would have provided for the applicant's private pay care. The transfer penalty period runs from the date of the transfer; there is no maximum disqualification period. The actions of one spouse are imputed to the other. In most cases, transfers within 36 months of application for Medicaid must be disclosed to the state Medicaid agency. Transfers to or from certain types of trusts must be disclosed on the Medicaid application if occurring within 60 months of application.

The transfer period is calculated in months, with a fractional month usually rounded down to the next whole month. The amount on which the transfer penalty is based may be a state supplied average monthly cost, or it may be the actual cost of the nursing home where you or your spouse lives.

EXAMPLE:

> Liz Dhole resides in KC Nursing Center where the cost of care is $3,000 per month. (Her state's transfer rule is based on the actual cost of care.) On January 1, 2004, her husband Bob Dhole, gave a gift of $15,000 to his friend, Newt Grinch. Assuming that in all other respects, Mrs. Dhole would qualify for assistance under the Medicaid program; this transfer will disqualify her until June 1, 2004. (Why? The $15,000 gift divided by $3,000/month cost = 5 months disqualification.)

As the above example illustrates, and contrary to popular belief, the disqualification period for transfers prior to February 2006, is not always a flat 36 months. It can be less. Many persons become confused, and assume that all transfers affect eligibility for the entire 36 months. The opposite is also true. At the same time, a large transfer can affect eligibility for longer than 36 months.

Certain transfers incur no penalty periods at all. We already noted that spouses can transfer assets between themselves. You can also transfer an asset if you receive fair market value for it. For example, if you take $50,000 from a bank account and buy an annuity with the funds, you may not incur any period of ineligibility. You can also convert "non-exempt" assets into "exempt" ones. If you take $30,000 from your savings account and pay off the mortgage on your home, you have not transferred an asset that will make you ineligible for Medicaid. You have simply converted a non-exempt asset (cash) into an exempt one (your home).

Once a person qualifies for Medicaid, there is no restriction on transfers of assets by her spouse. The general rule is that the community spouse resource allowance consists of assets that the spouse may use as he pleases.

EXAMPLE:

> Jennie Jones is in The Montel, a local nursing home. Jennie has qualified for Medicaid and her bills are being paid. Her spouse, Jerry Springer Jones now has title to the family home and $79,000 worth of bank accounts. Jerry transfers the home and all the cash to the couple's two children, Cavett and Carson. Jerry's transfer does not affect Jennie's continuing eligibility for assistance. However, if Jerry ever needs care in a nursing home, the transfers to Cavett and Carson will certainly affect his ability to obtain Medicaid.

For transfers of assets after February 2006, the rules are more draconian. You must now disclose transfers that occur within 60 months of applying for Medicaid. More importantly, transfers that have occurred within the prior 60 months now affect eligibility for the number of months the amount transferred would have paid for care, **beginning in the month in which the person applied for Medicaid** and not the month in which the transfer was made. The bottom line: what the rule attempts to do is make you wait 60 months after a transfer before applying for Medicaid.

Adding the asset transfer rules to the rules on assets and income completes the picture of how you could qualify for Medicaid to pay nursing home bills. Of the two government-funded healthcare programs discussed in this chapter, Medicare and Medicaid, only Medicaid provides any real funding for long-term healthcare needs. As we saw, Medicare does offer some limited short-term benefits that should not be ignored. A basic understanding of both the Medicare and Medicaid systems is necessary if you wish to protect and preserve your assets against the ravages of long-term care.

The rules in the Medicaid system vary greatly from state to state. The Medicaid system is constantly in a state of flux. Three separate governmental entities are involved in developing and administering the Medicaid program: the federal government, through Congressional legislation and through its financing of part of the program; each state's own legislation, which may tailor its laws within the federal guidelines; and the state agency that regulates the Medicaid program which usually publishes rules and regulations to aid caseworkers in interpreting the federal and state legislation. This chapter gives you a basic outline of the rules currently in effect. To protect assets against depletion from long-term care costs, you must understand and plan within the Medicaid rules. With these rules in mind, we next turn to the question of how to maximize preservation of assets while still qualifying yourself or your spouse for Medicaid. Our next chapters examine this and the preservation of your estate for your family as well.

13

Basic Training for the Front Lines— Examples of Medicaid Planning Strategies: Part I

As we described in our last chapter, the Medicaid system is one of the primary payors of long-term nursing home care in our country. Within certain limits, each state modifies the Medicaid rules that the federal government puts in place. Because of this, the ability to qualify for Medicaid assistance can vary from state to state. Further, the state agency administering the Medicaid program in your state may interpret the same federal statute or regulation differently.

In recent years, more individuals with immediate or imminent long-term care needs have been planning to gain Medicaid eligibility. Other persons are concerned about nursing home costs, but hope they never need to live in the "residence of last resort." Most of these are middle class couples who planned patiently for retirement. They are horrified at the prospect that costly nursing home care may wipe out a lifetime of savings in a few short months. These folks have looked to a variety of sources for assistance in planning for Medicaid to pay these costs. Books such as this one give background information. Friends and neighbors provide their own anecdotes about nursing home situations. Attorneys in many states now concentrate their practices in Medicaid planning. These lawyers offer their knowledge of the Medicaid rules as a help to plan financially for long-term healthcare needs.

This chapter begins our insight into the Medicaid planning process. Preliminary steps are examined. The next chapter will look at some basic Medicaid planning strategies. This chapter and the next are not going to provide you with an exact Medicaid plan for your situation. The area is complex and rapidly changing. An effective plan in one state may not work at all in another.

Regardless of where you live, the Medicaid planning process starts with three "pre-planning" steps:

1. You first need to have a basic knowledge of the five Medicaid rules we discussed in Chapter 12. Then you should gather together financial and other information on you and your family.

2. Next, you need to examine existing estate plans—wills, trusts, etc.—of all family members, including spouses and adult unmarried children.

3. Finally, you need to determine if Medicaid is a desirable option for you and your family. There are many reasons for not wanting to rely upon Medicaid for long-term care costs.

Assuming you understand the basic Medicaid rules, gathering family information comes first. Much like the traditional estate planning process, details on your family assets and finances, desired death beneficiaries, and the names of executors, trustees, or agents under powers of attorney are needed. Unlike traditional estate planning, however, other issues are present. What nursing homes are being considered, if any? Is the home a Medicaid-certified home? Will the home require that the resident demonstrate ability to private pay for a time? What is the anticipated monthly cost of the home? What is the competency level of the nursing home bound resident? Or, if neither you nor your spouse is nursing home bound, are there current medical conditions that may lead either of you to the nursing home in the near or long term future? Many of these additional issues are tough to sort out absent a crystal ball. Suppose your husband has Alzheimer's disease. This disease can progress at radically different rates in different people. How can you tell when he might need a nursing home? Some of the answers to these questions may be just your best guess or intuition.

If you are dealing with an imminent nursing home admission, a key to the early planning stages is the competency of the potential resident, his wishes, and ensuring that no one is pressuring him to plan. Medicaid planning is certainly unethical and probably illegal if it is done without the consent of the nursing home resident. Depending on how assets are titled, it may also be impossible. As you will see in the next chapter, shifting or changing the character or title of assets is the focus of almost every basic Medicaid plan. For example, if the family home is titled in joint tenancy, one spouse is clearly incompetent, and no powers of attorney or other planning has been done, how do you transfer the house title to the community spouse? This problem has its roots in the very first issue we discussed in this book: planning for incompetency. Medicaid planning may be possible on behalf of a now incompetent person if carefully drafted trusts or powers of attorney are already in existence.

Existing estate plans must be reviewed. You need to review the plans that you and your spouse have in effect. You also need to assess the plans of other family members. Why? Because if Medicaid is the payment method of choice for you or a family member, care should be exercised to ensure that no one leaves an outright bequest to the nursing home resident in his estate plan. In addition, a Medicaid recipient may be an heir of a family member with no formal estate plan. Intestacy laws must be checked.

EXAMPLE:

Bob Evans, a local pork farmer, contracted Alzheimer's disease. He is now a nursing home resident and is receiving Medicaid. His daughter, Dale Evans, is single and has a large estate. Dale has no descendants and dies, leaving no will. Her father Bob is an heir of her estate based on state intestacy laws. Bob inherits from his daughter, and the inheritance makes him ineligible for Medicaid.

Children, in particular, may have a Medicaid recipient as a natural heir of their estate. Children may also have named that person as a beneficiary of a formal estate plan. Another problem is how the community spouse should handle her estate plan. If the community spouse dies first, an inheritance left to the spouse in the nursing home jeopardizes continued Medicaid eligibility as well. Many community spouses would prefer to leave assets to children or other family members. As harsh as it seems, disinheritance of your nursing home spouse is a common and acceptable plan.

Disinheritance does not always work, however. In many states, the community spouse will have a claim filed against her estate or lien recorded against her house. In some states, the rights of the Medicaid agency to file a claim lie only against probate estates. In those states, the community spouse should take steps to be sure that her estate will not be probated. Thus, forms of holding title that avoid probate should be favored: trusts, joint tenancies (not with the spouse!), and direct death beneficiary designations.

Another glitch in a plan that disinherits a nursing home spouse is also contained in state law. In many states, you can disinherit your spouse, but he has a right to renounce the plan that does so. Upon renunciation, the spouse is then awarded an automatic share. For example, in most states, if you leave a will that makes no provision for your spouse, he can file a renunciation of the will. He then receives one-third of your estate. The rest of your estate is left to the people you named in the document.

Renunciation is a choice given your spouse. He could choose not to renounce your estate plan. So why is this a concern? It would seem logical that your spouse, if in a nursing home, will simply not exercise his rights to renounce. The inheritance should pass to your children.

Unfortunately, some states mandate that a Medicaid recipient exercise his right to renounce. Failure to do so is deemed a transfer of assets, subject to the transfer rule we looked at in Chapter 12. The failure to renounce can affect eligibility if it is deemed a disqualifying transfer.

Refusal to accept an inheritance is often a disqualifying transfer as well. In settings other than a Medicaid situation, people sometimes "disclaim" an inheritance. A "disclaimer" is a refusal to accept an inheritance. No one can force you to accept a gift you do not want! If you disclaim an inheritance, it passes as if you died before the decedent. Under Medicaid laws in many states, however, exercising a disclaimer can be viewed as a transfer of assets like a renunciation.

EXAMPLE:

Ken and Babs have been husband and wife for 50 years. Ken suffered a stroke that left him physically disabled, but mentally quite competent. He now lives in a nursing home. Ken and Babs have one daughter, Sheila. Misfortune seems to strike the family in threes. Shortly after Ken's stroke and admission into the nursing home, Babs and Sheila die simultaneously in a plane crash. Babs' will leaves all the family's assets, about $75,000, to charities. Sheila has no will, is not married and has no children, but has some assets of her own—around $50,000—from her successful career as a toy designer. Ken consults with his lawyer, Dewey C. Howe. Attorney Howe informs Ken that he has a right to renounce Babs' will and that he is the sole heir to Sheila's estate. Ken does not want to renounce Babs' will. He would also like to disclaim his interest in Sheila's estate. If Ken were to disclaim, the next heirs in line under state law for Sheila's estate would be Ken's nephews and nieces, who are favorites of Ken's. Attorney Howe breaks the bad news to Ken. If he disclaims the inheritance from Sheila, he will be deemed to have made a transfer in the amount of the inheritance. If he does not renounce Babs' will he will have made a second transfer. Ken could receive $50,000 from Sheila's estate. If he renounced Babs' will he would get 1/3 of her estate under local law, or $25,000. If he refuses to renounce Babs' will and disclaims his interest under Sheila's estate, he will have made a transfer totaling $75,000 between the two. The private pay cost for a bed in the nursing home where Ken resides is $2,500 per month. Thus, the transfers will make him ineligible for Medicaid for 30 months ($75,000 divided by $2,500 = 30).

If a family member other than a spouse wishes to remember the Medicaid recipient in an estate plan, sometimes a "supplemental needs trust" can be used. These trusts allow for payments for the benefit of the Medicaid recipient for supplemental needs only. Supplemental needs might be things such as clothing, snack foods, a television set, a companion, travel and other entertainment, and medical or dental procedures, which Medicaid does not cover. A supplemental needs trust can go a long way in making a nursing home resident's life more palatable. You need to check your state's law as to the Medicaid consequences of these trusts. In most states, however, a supplemental needs trust created by someone other than a spouse is viewed as an exempt asset. It will not affect eligibility.

EXAMPLE:

> Attorney Howe has some good news for Ken. Sheila did have an estate plan. She had created a supplemental needs trust that benefits Ken. Ken's nephew is the trustee of this trust. As trustee, Ken's nephew buys him clothing, a new TV for his room, and hires a counselor to help Ken through the grieving over the loss of his wife and daughter. This trust does not affect Ken's eligibility for Medicaid.

What about planning for the spouse of the Medicaid recipient? Can she disinherit her spouse and not affect his Medicaid eligibility? Three possible solutions exist for this problem.

The first solution is a strange quirk under Medicaid laws. Under the Medicaid system, you can have a will prepared that creates a trust within the will. A trust created under a will is called a "testamentary trust." The testamentary trust names your spouse in the nursing home as beneficiary. It should name another family member or perhaps a bank or trust company as trustee. The testamentary trust is created as a supplemental needs trust. While under Medicaid rules you cannot create a living trust that is a supplemental needs trust for the benefit of your spouse, you are permitted to do so in a testamentary trust. Properly drafted, this testamentary trust will provide for your spouse but not affect continuing Medicaid eligibility.

What is the downside to a testamentary supplemental needs trust? At first glance this plan seems more acceptable than a harsh disinheritance of your spouse. What are the drawbacks?

First, because it is a testamentary trust, it does not exist during your lifetime. It exists only under your will. A will does nothing while you are alive. The will comes into play only after death. It is the will that creates the testamentary supplemental needs trust. For your will to dispose of significant assets, it must be probated. Thus, if you want to create a testamentary supplemental needs trust to benefit your nursing home spouse, plan on your estate being probated.

Secondly, the testamentary supplemental needs trust is "born" in probate court. It will provide for contingent beneficiaries (your children or family) if your spouse predeceases you or if he or she later dies. The drawback is that upon the death of your spouse, or upon your death, if your spouse died first, the probate estate gives the state Medicaid agency an easy route to file an estate claim. The estate claim will diminish or eliminate any inheritance passing to other family members.

Third and finally, the testamentary supplemental needs trust does not seem a logical fit under the Medicaid rules. As mentioned above, it is a somewhat quirky exception. Many commentators believe that this exception may be legislated out of existence under future changes in Medicaid laws. As a result, few attorneys in the Medicaid planning field utilize testamentary supplemental needs trusts. Why use an exception that is very vulnerable to changes in the law?

A change in the Medicaid laws may not impact the second alternative that the community spouse may choose. Remember in our last chapter we looked at "post eligibility" transfers. After the spouse in the nursing home qualifies for Medicaid, the community spouse can gift her assets. These gifts do not affect the eligibility of the nursing home spouse to continue to receive Medicaid. Of course, if she makes significant gifts, the community spouse is gambling that she will not need nursing home care herself in the next five years. Significant gifts will probably make the community spouse ineligible for Medicaid for the entire five-year look back period.

EXAMPLE:

> Ken and Babs, husband and wife, have one adult daughter, Sheila. Ken enters the nursing home. After spending the family funds on private pay care for a time, Babs and Ken apply for Medicaid to pay Ken's nursing home bills. Babs has $101,640 plus the family home, which the state allows her to keep as a community spouse. Ken becomes eligible for Medicaid and the state begins to pay his cost of care. Babs is in good health. She decides to transfer the home and the $101,640 to Sheila. These transfers do not affect Ken's ability to continue to receive Medicaid. If Babs needs a nursing home in the next five years, she will have made transfers that may prohibit her from receiving Medicaid. However, when Babs and Ken pass away, neither of them have any estate against which the state Medicaid agency can file a claim. Sheila's "inheritance"—the gifted assets—are preserved for her.

There are drawbacks to giving away all the community spouse assets. In our example above, what if Sheila gets divorced, is sued, or has a problem with creditors? Babs' assets will be exposed to these problems. If the family home or the other assets have appreciated in value since Ken and Babs purchased them, Sheila may pay a hefty capital gains tax when she sells them. If Babs received any breaks on her property taxes on her home—a senior citizen exemption or a reduction because it is her residence—those breaks will disappear now that Sheila owns the home. Perhaps the biggest drawback to giving away all the family assets is loss of income and control. Babs may need the income or access to her money to survive. Babs may also feel uncomfortable about placing all her "eggs in one basket," that is into Sheila's hands.

A third alternative is creating a trust that names Babs as a beneficiary. Two types of trusts are possible.

The first type of trust is one we have already discussed. If the community spouse gifts all her assets to a child, can the child in turn take those assets and create a supplemental needs trust for the benefit of the parent? In some states this seems to be acceptable. In others, the state Medicaid agency will consider the supplemental needs trust as being funded with the parent's assets and not the child's. It will ignore the gift as "form over substance," and follow the basic rule that you cannot create a trust with your own assets to protect these assets from your creditors. Remember the statute of Elizabeth we discussed several chapters ago? The state agency may view a gift to a child followed by creation of a supplemental needs trust to violate the statute of Elizabeth. This is yet another case where you need to check how your state would view this transaction.

EXAMPLE:

> In the state where Ken and Babs live, a gift to a child who then creates a supplemental needs trust is acceptable. After Ken gains Medicaid eligibility for his nursing care, Babs transfers her home and $101,640 to Sheila. Sheila creates a supplemental needs trust that will provide for Babs' needs.

The supplemental needs trust helps with one drawback to the gifting of community spouse assets. It allows the community spouse to have some access to the income and assets on which she may live. The supplemental needs trust is still exposed to Sheila's potential problems with creditors, divorcing spouses, or lawsuits. It does not alleviate any capital gains tax problems. It does not restore any property tax exemptions that Babs once enjoyed. It still makes Babs ineligible for Medicaid for up to five years. It does however, protect the assets against estate claims from the state Medicaid agency when Babs or Ken dies.

Another type of trust that Babs could consider is an asset protection trust. This is one trust that we have not yet discussed. It is a sophisticated and complex tool. We will examine in more detail how it operates in chapter 15. The asset protection trust allows the surviving spouse to be a direct beneficiary. No gifts are made to children. It retains any tax advantages on real estate, eliminates the capital gains tax problems that occur if gifts are made, and does not expose assets to the problems of your children or other heirs to your estate. The asset protection trust is a flexible and useful tool for the community spouse. It is created with the assets that the community spouse may keep.

EXAMPLE:

> Back to poor Ken and Babs. Ken has entered the nursing home, and Medicaid is now paying the bills. Babs has kept the family home and $101,640 in bank accounts. With the assistance of clever attorney Matt Tell, Babs creates an asset protection trust. The trust will help support her. It allows her to live in her home, or to sell the home if she desires. The trust assets may be sheltered if Babs needs care in a nursing home after five years. She is gambling that she will stay healthy and not need care during that time.

The asset protection trust, gifts, or gifts with creation of a supplemental needs trust are three estate plans the community spouse can consider. We have also seen how children or other family members who want to remember a Medicaid recipient in their estate plans should consider creating supplemental needs trusts. In these discussions, we have assumed that having Medicaid pay the bills is a good thing. In our next chapter, we will look at how we can retain larger amounts of assets and qualify a person for Medicaid sooner. Some folks, however, may prefer to private pay longer, avoiding Medicaid altogether.

Private pay may be a better approach for those who believe that Medicaid is welfare. Some believe strongly that welfare is for those who cannot afford to pay and not for those who can afford to plan. Others believe that nursing homes treat Medicaid recipients different from private pay residents. They believe that a Medicaid recipient receives poorer quality care. Some may resent government interference into their affairs. The Medicaid application process is an intrusive, often frustrating ordeal. Finally, the more able you are to pay privately, the more choices of nursing homes you have. Some nursing homes do not accept Medicaid at all. Others discriminate prior to admitting someone. If you cannot pay for a long time on your own, a nursing home can legally refuse to admit you.

Despite these cautions, many still want to forge ahead. In our next chapter, we will look at ways in which you and your family can preserve more assets while still qualifying for Medicaid. We can legally increase some of the limits the law places on assets retained by a community spouse. We do so by taking advantage of the planning options in the Medicaid laws.

14

Basic Training for the Front Lines— Examples of Medicaid Planning Strategies: Part II

You reviewed your estate plan, the plans of your spouse and children, and possibly your parents. You or your spouse (or parent) has been admitted to or is shortly going to enter a nursing home. As best you can, you think you have a handle on the basic Medicaid rules we looked at in Chapter 12. Now the Medicaid planning process can begin in earnest.

Because Medicaid laws can change rapidly, and without much advance notice, you need know that Medicaid planning is not guaranteed. It is truly more art than science. If you do a Medicaid plan, it may not be "grandfathered" under new Medicaid laws or changes in current law. As states deal with budget constraints, many view the Medicaid program as an area to "tighten the belt."

Moreover, significant changes occurred in the federal Medicaid laws in February of 2006. As each state passes its own regulations to implement these changes, the situation will likely be confusing for some time to come. As we look at Medicaid plans in this chapter, we will highlight what works under pre-February, 2006 rules and how the new law may affect a planning option from that point forward.

Many lawyers and others who counsel persons on Medicaid try to offer clients several options. You may choose to visit an elder law attorney, a social worker, an accountant, or financial planner for assistance. You will find that there is not a "one size fits all" Medicaid plan. Suggested plans may range from fairly conservative approaches that are as close to tried and true as possible, to aggressive—and risky—Medicaid planning that may tempt state denials of coverage and appeals. Ultimately, the choice of what option to pursue, if any, is up to you!

As we have discussed earlier, the Medicaid rules are a hybrid of state and federal law. Each state has an agency in charge of running the Medicaid program. State laws and the interpretation of federal laws by the state Medicaid agencies vary greatly. Because Medicaid planning is very state specific, you need to exercise additional care. The purpose of this chapter is to offer you some insights into the Medicaid planning process. The following are generic plans that may or may not work in your state.

Enough cautions? The purpose in cautioning you is not to discourage you from Medicaid planning. Many engage in Medicaid planning and most are quite successful. You need to be aware of the risks. Often, however, the "failure" of a Medicaid plan leaves you no worse off than had you not tried in the first place. With the cost of nursing homes rocketing towards $8,000 per month and higher, it is a very cost effective type of planning.

This chapter will look at eight basic Medicaid strategies. The eight we will examine are: divorce, "just say no," increasing the community spouse resource allowance, annuities, self-canceling installment notes, conversion of non-exempt assets into exempt, gifts, and the use of trusts. Sometimes, more than one strategy is used simultaneously in formulating an effective plan. We will "rate" each plan according to the approximate risk involved and if the plan may work as an asset protection tool. One star (*) means the plan is very risky; four stars (****) means the plan is as close to tried and true as we have in this area. As you might guess, two stars (**) is a fairly risky technique, while three stars (***) is a fairly conservative one.

Our first Medicaid plan is a simple, straightforward, and often horrifying approach: the Medicaid divorce. Most persons who have been happily (or tolerably) married for 40, 50, or even 60 years automatically rebel at the idea of divorce. Social, religious, and emotional reasons prevent divorce from being a popular Medicaid plan. Divorce tends to be a better alternative in situations where spouses have long since separated, but never formally divorced. In most states, even if you and your spouse separated years ago, you are still responsible for each other's debts and nursing home care.

Divorce does work as a Medicaid plan. Divorcing spouses can agree to a division of assets and sign a settlement agreement. Courts usually do not disturb agreements about splitting assets that spouses work out. The divorce is finalized by a court order. This order not only ends the marriage, but also confirms the settlement agreement that splits the assets. The state Medicaid agency will honor the division of assets confirmed in the court order. Equally important, a split of assets between spouses under a court order is not considered a transfer that results in any penalty period under Medicaid laws.

In the Medicaid divorce, assets are transferred to the healthy spouse. The amount of assets can be in excess of what the spouse would normally be allowed to keep under the spousal allowance. The court order in the divorce approves the split, and the healthy spouse keeps the assets. The spouse in the nursing home could become Medicaid eligible shortly or even immediately.

With the healthy spouse no longer married to a Medicaid recipient, the assets are also safe from liens and estate claims. Thus, the assets in the hands of the healthy spouse are also preserved as future inheritances for children and family.

EXAMPLE:

Donald and Ivana have been married for many years. Donald is physically quite ill and enters Atlantic City Nursing Center. Together, Donald and Ivana own a house worth about $150,000 and $350,000 in cash, stocks and bonds. In the state where they live, Ivana will be allowed to keep the house and $101,640 in other assets while Donald receives Medicaid. Until that time, however, Ivana must spend the rest of the assets on private pay nursing care. Of the $350,000 in cash and securities, about $250,000 would be consumed. Donald and Ivana retain separate lawyers to begin divorce proceedings. Donald agrees to give the house and $300,000 to Ivana in the divorce. He will keep $50,000. The court enters an order dissolving the marriage and approving the division of the assets. Donald, as a single person, buys a pre-paid funeral plan, sets aside $2,000 in an account, and spends the rest of his funds on the nursing home. He then becomes eligible for Medicaid. Ivana retains the house and $300,000. She places them into a living trust that will leave them to the couples' children when she dies. The house and other assets will not be subjected to any estate claims or liens because Ivana is not Donald's spouse. The divorce saved Donald and Ivana $200,000. Instead of spending $250,000 on private pay nursing care, Donald spent his $50,000.

Divorce might be a more difficult plan if a healthy spouse wants to institute proceedings against a nursing home bound spouse of dubious competency. A guardian may be appointed to represent the incompetent spouse. The guardian will be obligated to protect as many assets as possible for the disabled spouse. A guardianship judge will have to approve any divorce plan that divides assets. The judge may be zealous in "protecting" assets for the incompetent spouse. She may not allow a disproportionate split of assets.

If a power of attorney is in place appointing an agent for an incompetent spouse, a court may allow the agent to represent the spouse in a divorce. This would eliminate the need for a guardian. Obviously, if the power of attorney named the other spouse as agent, he or she would have to resign and let the next named agent in the document act. The conflict of having an agent who also happens to be suing the principal for divorce would not be allowed! Assume you want to divorce your husband. He is now incompetent. He has a power of attorney naming you as his agent and your son as successor agent. You may be able to divorce without a guardian involved, using the power of attorney. However, you would have to resign as agent and let your son act.

Assuming that you either have a competent spouse or a power of attorney that will allow someone to act on behalf of a spouse in a divorce, this option is a conservative one: Four stars (****).

In some states, spouses have refused to care for one another, and refused to pay for private pay care, forcing the Medicaid issue. This is our second plan. With apologies to the anti-drug crusaders, many have termed this the "just say no" approach. This is a risky tactic that seems to be fraught with dangers, yet some states, such as New York and Illinois, appear to permit it, although Illinois is presently contemplating eliminating this provision. Other states, however, have statutes that render both spouses liable for these types of debts.

Why does the "just say no approach" exist in the first place? It is there because states needed to deal with the issue of the missing spouse. Suppose your spouse abandoned you years ago. You now enter a nursing home and have no clue where your spouse could be found. Your state may have Medicaid regulations that allow you to consider yourself as an unmarried person. The presumption is that your missing spouse is uncooperative. The Medicaid laws do not penalize you for your spouse's lack of cooperation.

The states that do allow the "just say no" approach phrase their regulations in terms of spouses who refuse to cooperate. The regulations state that if you have a spouse that does not cooperate, you are treated as if you were unmarried. Thus, of the assets that you have, you would be allowed to claim just $2,000, your personal effects, and a burial plan as exempt assets. Your "uncooperative" spouse, of course, keeps all the assets she has in her name.

The "just say no" approach may only work if a couple has had separately titled assets. It probably will not be a viable alternative if you and your spouse own everything jointly, split your assets, and shortly after apply for Medicaid. This plan may have a high reward, like divorce. It allows the healthy spouse to keep all her solely owned assets. The potential reward comes with a high risk: One star (*).

As you should remember (refer to Chapter 12 if you don't) we have two community spouse allowances permitted under the rules. One deals with income. The other deals with assets. What if the community spouse's income, together with the institutionalized spouse's income, and the income generated by the assets permitted under the state's community spouse resource allowance, is insufficient to produce the state's community spouse income allowance? Can you ask to keep more assets so that you can produce more income from those assets? In most states, the community spouse can petition the state agency to allow a greater community spouse resource allowance. This is our third planning strategy.

EXAMPLE:

Jack Cassity and wife Shirley are a happily married couple. Jack, however, had to enter The Family Nursing Center. Shirley would be a community spouse when Jack applies for Medicaid. Her state allows a resource allowance of $101,640 and income of $2,541 per month. All the couples' assets are invested in bank accounts that pay about 5% interest per year. Shirley receives social security of $450 per month. Jack, the institutionalized spouse, receives social security and a musician's pension totaling $1100 per month. If Shirley was allowed to retain only $101,640 in assets, with a 5% return, the assets would generate only another $420 per month in income. The total monthly income possible for Shirley under this scenario is $1970 per month ($420 bank interest plus her income of $450 plus Jack's of $1100). Furthermore, if Jack dies and Shirley does not receive any of Jack's pension, her income will fall even lower. Shirley could petition her state agency to allow her to retain more than $101,640 in community spouse resources to "boost" her income to $2,541 per month. She needs another $571 a month. At around 5% interest, she would ask the state to allow her an additional $137,000 in assets. A total spousal allowance of $238,000 brings her $941 per month in interest income. Add that to the couples' regular income, and she will be close to her spousal allowance of $2,541. Her two sons, David and Jack Jr., urge her to do just that.

In many states, California being a prime example, this is a highly effective Medicaid plan. Depending upon the state, it may not be a particularly high-risk approach, however. All you need to do is file your Medicaid application earlier than normal. If the state denies your request for an increased spousal allowance, you should be able to simply withdraw your Medicaid application and move on to another planning approach. In our example above, Shirley and Jack could apply for Medicaid when their assets equal $238,000, they would petition to keep those assets. The worst thing that might happen is a denial of Medicaid coverage. They could then withdraw their application and try one of the other approaches mentioned in this chapter. Other states, however, require you to go to court to obtain a court order permitting a higher spousal allowance. If the court agrees, and allows the higher amount, the state Medicaid agency will follow this ruling. There is a risk that the judge may not allow this, and you would be out the attorney's fees for this proceeding.

How does this approach rate? While not always successful, the "failure" of this plan should leave you no worse off than had you not tried at all: Three stars (***).

Our fourth plan is a favorite of many asset protection planners. In the past, when Congress has changed the Medicaid laws, they severely restricted the use of trusts. From time to time, Congress tried to similarly hamper another popular Medicaid planning tool, the annuity. Despite a strong lobbying effort by insurance companies, Congress succeeded with the February 2006 changes that severely weakened the uses of annuities as weapons in the asset protection arsenal.

What is an annuity? In simple terms, an annuity is an agreement with a company or individual to pay you a periodic return of your investment plus a rate of return, over your lifetime or a period of years. Annuities can accrue interest prior to the regular payments beginning. Alternatively, you can buy an immediate annuity, which begins periodic payments at once. For Medicaid purposes, the immediate annuity is the investment of choice.

Most annuities are sold by insurance companies. While not insured by the federal government like a bank account, they are considered a very safe investment when bought from a stable, reputable company. You can also create a private annuity arrangement with children or other family members. The annuity is a contract and as such, you are bound by its terms. How does an immediate annuity work as a Medicaid plan? Once an annuity begins periodic payments, you cannot surrender it and receive your investment back. What the annuity provides you is the right to payments every month or quarter. When properly structured, the annuity is an asset that is unavailable to you. The payments are treated as income. You have taken an asset and turned it into an income stream for Medicaid purposes. (The purists among you will note that the payments from an annuity are not all income for income tax purposes!) Unless you live in a income cap state, the payments do not affect eligibility. In addition, if you follow Medicaid guidelines, the annuity is not a transfer of assets. It does not create any ineligibility period because your purchase of an annuity is a fair market value transaction.

What should you look for in an annuity policy? Five features are necessary. First, the annuity contract must state that you cannot surrender the annuity once you begin receiving monthly or quarterly payments. Second, the annuity should pay to the community spouse, not to the spouse in the nursing home. Third, the annuity contract must state that it cannot be sold, transferred or assigned. Fourth, the annuity must be "actuarially sound." The annuity cannot be for a term of years that is longer than the community spouse's life expectancy under government published tables. Fifth, you must purchase the policy with a single premium, that is, with one lump payment of cash.

EXAMPLE:

> Assume that Babe Ruth is a nursing home resident. Her state allows a community spouse resource allowance of $101,640. Her husband George, has cash or other non-exempt assets totally $120,000. George purchases a single premium commercial annuity for $19,000. The annuity annuitizes immediately (i.e. makes quarterly payments), and George cannot access the principal in the annuity. The income is payable directly to him. George is 75 years old, and the annuity is for a 10-year term. The government life expectancy tables list a life expectancy of greater than 10 years for a 75-year-old male. Babe applies for Medicaid. What result? Under the rules it appears George made a transfer, but not a disqualifying one, because he purchased something for fair market value, the annuity. Nevertheless, the principal of the annuity is inaccessible for Babe's care, as the annuity cannot be cashed. Babe should then be approved for Medicaid assistance immediately.

A variation on the annuity approach is the private annuity. What if an annuity contract is prepared and executed not with a commercial insurance company, but with another family member? Would the result be any different from how a commercial annuity is viewed? In some states, attorneys are successfully using private annuity contracts with family members instead of looking to commercial insurance company annuities.

States are looking harder at annuities, despite the best efforts of the insurance industry to lobby otherwise. Wisconsin has already promulgated rules to declare an annuity a disqualifying transfer. Illinois has threatened to follow. It remains to be seen whether this will survive a court challenge or if other states follow.

The February, 2006 changes add that an annuity, unless it is a "qualified annuity" (more about that in a moment), must also make the state the first remainder beneficiary upon the death of the owner. Essentially, the annuity is then paid back to the state if the owner dies before it has completed its schedule of regular payments. This restricts the use of annuities as methods to protect an inheritance for children or other family members.

One useful exception to the February, 2006 law is if the annuity is a "qualified annuity." A qualified annuity is one purchased with tax-deferred funds: the money comes from something like an IRA account or a 401(k) plan.

Whether qualified or non-qualified, it is critical that any annuity, meets the five criteria listed above. If you structure an annuity properly, <u>and</u> under the new rules, the monies used to purchase the annuity come from an IRA or similar plan, you may have a very effective Medicaid protection plan. I would rate it as only two stars because too many persons do not purchase an annuity carefully and miss one or more of the five criteria, or do not have tax-deferred accounts available to use for its purchase, making the annuity vulnerable. Two stars (**).

An interesting variant on the annuity idea is a self-canceling installment note. This is our fifth Medicaid plan. You may see these instruments referred to as a "SCIN" in articles or other books. Like an annuity, if you loan someone money, and he or she pays you back over time, you have changed an asset to an income stream for Medicaid purposes. If the person to whom you loaned the money signs a promissory note to pay you in regular installments, you can create an exempt asset.

The note must meet many of the same requirements as an annuity. You must not be able to sell or assign the note. It must pay to the community spouse. It should be a single loan transaction of a lump sum, not amounts given out a little at a time. The note should bear a reasonable market rate of interest, i.e., you cannot have a promissory note bearing 0% interest.

To whom do you loan the money? Usually to your children. As an added bonus, you make the note cancel upon your death. The note then "disappears" from your estate and is no longer an asset exposed to estate claims. In return for this feature, you should set the interest rate one or two percentage points higher than what a reasonable market rate would be. Sound confusing? Let's look at an example:

EXAMPLE:

Jimmy and Rosalind own a home and have $200,000 in bank accounts. They have one child, daughter Amy. Jimmy suffers from dementia. Jimmy is admitted to The Georgian Rest Home, a nursing facility. In the state where Jimmy and Rosalind live, Rosalind is permitted to keep the family home and $101,640 in cash as a community spouse without affecting Jimmy's eligibility for Medicaid. Rosalind loans $98,000 to Amy. Amy signs a promissory note saying she will pay Rosalind the $98,000 back with 10 years of monthly payments. Amy will pay Rosalind 6% interest on the loan. The note cannot be sold or transferred by Rosalind unless Amy agrees. The note and any interest will be automatically forgiven if Rosalind dies before it is paid back. Jimmy applies for Medicaid. The state views Rosalind as having three exempt assets: the house, $101,640 in cash, and the note from Amy. Jimmy has $2,000, which is also exempt for him. As a bonus, if Rosalind dies, the note is forgiven, and the money that Amy still has not repaid her is Amy's to keep. It cannot be used to pay any estate claim that the state may file against Rosalind's estate.

One unknown feature of a SCIN is if the length of the loan has to be actuarially sound, like an annuity. In other words, could a 75-year-old man loan money to a child with a 30-year repayment schedule? This is not an actuarially sound loan, because the life expectancy tables would say that an average 75-year-old male will not live to age 105. It seems that no state has any specific regulations requiring that a SCIN be actuarially sound. However, many attorneys who prepare these documents for clients assume that the SCIN should make sense in terms of the lender's life expectancy. For a 75-year-old male, for example, an attorney might suggest a 10 or 12-year loan.

The SCIN also avoids estate claims, because the note extinguishes at death. With the note gone, the state cannot compel the borrower to repay the deceased lender's estate. Thus, any funds remaining that have not been repaid are protected.

Based on the foregoing, doesn't this sound like a great Medicaid plan? Congress agreed, and in February 2006, re-defined SCINs as disqualifying transfers of assets. Therefore, unless a SCIN already exists from a transaction that occurred prior to 2006, the SCIN is now useless as a Medicaid tool. Zero stars (0).

Suppose our friends in the last example, Rosalind and Jimmy, had a $98,000 mortgage on their home. If Rosalind and Jimmy pay off the mortgage with some of their cash, and then apply for Medicaid, what is the result? Jimmy should qualify. A conversion of a non-exempt asset (the excess cash) into an exempt asset (the house) is permitted. This is our sixth Medicaid plan and a very effective one if not done to excess. The same result would be achieved for Jimmy and family if they sold their existing home, and purchased a more expensive one, or spent money to repair the existing residence. On a smaller scale, this works with purchase of graves, grave markers, or other exempt assets.

We offer a word of caution in using this technique. Many state agencies will be mindful of abuses of this technique. For example, while wedding rings are exempt, the purchase by Jimmy and Rosalind of a new, $70,000 set might be heavily scrutinized. In addition, while payment of needed housing expenses is permissible, expensive improvements may not be. Replacement of an old, leaky roof is permissible; installing a $70,000 swimming pool in the back yard might not be!

This Medicaid planning technique is a matter of course, if your assets are minimal. Purchase a burial lot and a pre-paid funeral. Plan to ensure that the minimal amounts of cash allotted to a Medicaid resident is retained by applying for Medicaid on a timely basis.

Another restriction on this plan added in 2006 is that the equity in the family home can no longer exceed $500,000. States can opt to increase this equity limit, but in no event to an amount over $750,000. As states begin to pass regulations to implement this part of the federal law, it seems as if claiming a house as an exempt asset may become a battle of the appraisals. You, as a Medicaid applicant, will want a low valuation on your home. The state will believe it to be worth more.

Despite the new equity restrictions, and assuming that you don't go crazy and buy $70,000 worth of wedding rings, have a high value residence or abuse this technique in a similar manner, this is a good, solid Medicaid plan. Four stars (****).

Remember our 60-month transfer rule? Assuming that you can wait until any disqualification period has run, or in any event no longer than 60 months, transfers can work to shelter some assets while qualifying you or your spouse for Medicaid sooner. The technique of outright gifting is plan number seven on our list. It is particularly appropriate where the potential Medicaid recipient is single and makes a competent, informed choice to gift. Be careful, however, about gifting assets that are highly appreciated property. This will cause capital gain tax consequences to the recipient. In addition, beware of the child who desires to gift a parent's assets to qualify for Medicaid under the guise of "because Dad wanted it this way." Is this really Dad's choice, or is a "benevolent" child stripping Dad of his assets?

Gifts are a radical solution. They strip you of the ability to use your assets. They deprive you of the income the assets generate. It may also be difficult to calculate how much money to gift and how much to retain, as care needs and costs can change suddenly and substantially. For many, however, gifts are probably the first thing that comes to mind. Many older adults facing a nursing home situation have good, trustworthy children upon whom they can rely.

Another problem that gifts create even with the most angelic of children is unforeseen problems that befall the child. What if you make a sizable gift to a child, and then he later goes through divorce proceedings, gets sued, or runs afoul of creditors? Your gift is now your child's asset and can be used to satisfy his soon-to-be ex-spouse, or any type of judgment. One way to look at gifts to children is to ask the child to voluntarily place the assets into an asset protection trust. We have touched upon this type of trust earlier. We will look at it in greater detail in our next chapter. The asset protection trust would help insulate the gifted assets from these concerns.

Assuming that you get competent expert advice on how to create a gifting plan, this strategy should present you with an lower than average amount of risk. Three stars (***).

Our last plan to which we look for asset protection is the use of trusts. Trusts may be coupled with gifts to children, or may be created either by a single person or married couple. The use of trusts as a Medicaid plan has been curtailed over recent years. Basically, we have two choices you can consider that involve a trust.

Keep in mind that a direct transfer to a trust results in a 60-month look back period. If you and your advisors can work the math, you could create a Medicaid trust, wait out a period of disqualification, and the assets within the trust will be sheltered. What is a Medicaid trust? Basically, a Medicaid trust has four primary features. First, it allows you or your spouse to receive only income. You can never access the principal of the trust. Second, it must be an irrevocable trust. What this means is that once this document is created, you can never change or revoke it. Third, you should follow a conservative approach and make this trust a trust agreement and not a declaration of trust. In other words, pick someone besides you or your spouse to be trustee. Fourth, provide death beneficiaries in the trust that inherit the assets when you die, but reserve the right to yourself or your spouse to change the death beneficiaries by a provision in your will. This right is called a "limited power of appointment." The limited power of appointment, while too complicated to explain in detail here, provides significant capital gains tax relief to family members who might inherit from the trust. It does not take away from our basic requirement that in all other respects, the trust is irrevocable.

EXAMPLE:

> Frank Synatra Sr. has a home and about $500,000 in the bank. His wife, Nancy, suffers from dementia and may need a nursing home. Frank Sr. creates an irrevocable trust naming his son, Frank, Jr., as trustee. The trust is funded with $300,000 in cash. The trust pays the income only to Frank Sr.; he can never get at the principal. Frank Jr. invests the money carefully, earning 6% income on it. At that rate, the $300,000 trust pays Frank Sr. $18,000 per year. The trust leaves all the assets to Frank Jr. upon Frank Sr.'s death. But Frank Sr. could change the death beneficiary if he wants. Assuming that $200,000 will cover Nancy's nursing home bills for at least 60 months, the trust fund will be safe, and Frank Sr. will have the income to live on the rest of his life.

One big drawback to the Medicaid trust is that it may be vulnerable to estate claims. In our example above, if Nancy qualifies for Medicaid, and Frank Sr. dies, the trust may have to pay an estate claim before Frank Jr. receives his inheritance.

The other trust you could use is the asset protection trust, coupled with a gift to children. Remember the supplemental needs trust? Your children could create an asset protection trust that is also a supplemental needs trust for you. In this way, your children may have more access to assets than a Medicaid trust, where you are restricted to income only.

The Medicaid trust is a safe if somewhat limited plan. With the specter of a 60-month window, few may have sufficient assets to consider this tool. It may be best suited when you have a spouse or single person whom is fairly young, with a potentially lengthy stay in a nursing home ahead. Suppose your spouse is only 63 years old, physically as strong as an ox, but already impaired mentally. He could be spending 10 or more years in a nursing home. If you have significant assets to protect, a 60-month wait for Medicaid may be worth it. The other problem of the Medicaid trust is the potential exposure to estate claims. This trust may not protect assets once both spouses are gone.

A gift to children who voluntarily create an asset protection trust that provides supplemental needs benefits to you is perhaps more useful. This is also a fairly safe approach to the Medicaid process assuming that your state has not nixed this idea.

Both trust plans, if structured correctly, provide an effective Medicaid plan. Three stars (***).

Medicaid planning is controversial, risky, and fraught with tough decisions. It can also be one of the most cost-effective forms of estate planning. This chapter gave you some basic ideas on eight approaches Medicaid planners use. Further, you can often combine plans into one comprehensive strategy. Finally, in conjunction with a skilled Medicaid planning professional, there are undoubtedly other plans that can be formulated.

15

What About the Children? Protecting the Inheritance in Medicaid Planning

As we have seen in our last chapter, there are a variety of ways to "create" Medicaid eligibility while still protecting assets. You or your spouse, working within the rules, can shelter additional assets with Medicaid planning. We now turn to one additional goal in the Medicaid planning process: protecting assets for future generations.

As we learned in Chapter 12, the state has two ways to seek reimbursement of benefits that are provided to you or your spouse under the Medicaid program. The state can lien your residence. The state can file a claim against the estate of you or your spouse upon death. Neither of these methods seeking reimbursement directly affect you or your spouse while alive. However, liens and estate claims clearly reduce or eliminate any inheritance you may choose to pass on to your children, other family members, or even charities.

How much will the estate claim or lien total? Your state will pay for care in the nursing home, as well as certain other medical expenses. The rate at which the state pays is not the same as the private pay rate. Instead, it is based upon a formula that the Medicaid regulations will provide. It can be difficult to accurately predict the total amount paid. A good rule of thumb for the basic reimbursement rate for the nursing home services, however, is about 70% of the private pay rate. Thus, if the nursing home you reside in charges $5,000 per month to private pay residents, the nursing home will be paid around $3,500 per month for Medicaid reimbursement. Any income that you have that you are required to pay towards cost of care reduces the amount the state will pay. Remember our basic income rules? If you are single, all your income except for $30 per month goes to cost of care. If you are married, your spouse receives the spousal allowance from income, and less (or maybe none) of your income will be used towards cost of care.

EXAMPLE:

> Frank enters Pennsylvania Nursing Castle and qualifies for Medicaid. Frank has income of $1,000 per month from social security. His wife, Irene, has income of $800 per month from her social security. They are quite poor and have almost no assets. The state where Frank and Irene live provides a spousal income allowance of $2,541 per month. The private pay rate at Pennsylvania Nursing Castle is $3,600 per month, and the Medicaid reimbursement rate is $2,400 per month. When Frank qualifies for Medicaid, all his income is given to Irene as a spousal allowance. This gives Irene income of $1,800 per month, which is still under the spousal income allowance. The state is then paying the $2,400 per month reimbursement rate to the nursing home for his care. After 12 months of Medicaid care, Frank is surviving quite well in the nursing home, but Irene dies. Now Frank is single. All but $30 of his $1,000 monthly income goes towards cost of care—$970. Now the state is providing $1,430 per month reimbursement ($2,400—$970 = $1430). Frank lives another 12 months in the nursing home and then dies. The total amount of assistance the state provided him is $45,960. This is calculated on 12 months paying in full ($2400 x 12 months = $28,000), plus 12 months paying the reimbursement rate less what Frank's income provides ($2400—$970 x 12 months = $17,160), for a total of $45,960 ($28,000 + $17,160).

The claim that the state may have can rise quickly. The claim can easily total $20—45,000 per year of assistance. So if you receive Medicaid for three or four years, your estate can owe $75-180,000 or more to satisfy a Medicaid claim!

The claim can severely diminish your ability to leave an inheritance to children or other family. It may be large enough to wipe out your entire estate. Some of the techniques we examined in the last chapter will avoid estate claims. You can gift money to children, or loan it to them and in return receive a self-canceling installment note (SCIN), if done prior to the 2006 changes. However, each of these strategies places your money into the hands of your children. Your assets are now exposed to your children's problems: their divorces, creditors or lawsuits. Absent additional planning, the only sure way to protect assets from an estate claim and also protect them from dilemmas your children may face is to divorce your spouse. This is perhaps our least popular Medicaid plan.

We have an additional tool that we can couple with some of our basic Medicaid planning strategies to preserve inheritances. The asset protection trust, ("APT") mentioned briefly in previous chapters, is a device that can avoid estate claims. It may be used in one of two ways.

The first way you might use an APT is if you are married. A married couple would first plan to create more assets to support the healthy spouse. You might purchase an annuity, or try to create more exempt assets, or petition your state to allow the healthy spouse more assets to generate an income allowance. Once the institutionalized spouse qualifies for Medicaid, the healthy spouse places virtually all her assets into the APT. This trust allows her access to the assets for the rest of her life but is not as vulnerable to estate claims.

Another way you can use an APT will work whether you are single or married. In this case, you elect as a basic planning option to gift assets to family members. To protect assets from problems befalling the family members, they voluntarily create an APT and place assets into the trust. You no longer have direct control or access to these assets, but may retain some limited rights, as we will see. You must keep in mind, of course, that some states will not allow voluntarily created trusts, viewing these (perhaps rightfully) as a trust that still contains "your" assets. You would need to know your state's view of this plan.

What is an APT? How does it work? How does it fulfill our needs as a tool in the asset protection area as a Medicaid planning device for middle class America?

An APT differs from the typical revocable living trust we looked at in Chapters 7 and 8. It has five features that when made a part of your Medicaid plan, lessen vulnerability to estate claims:

1. The APT gives the trustee absolute discretion to distribute income and principal to you, your spouse, or to your children.

2. The APT tempers this power of the trustee by providing another individual, called a "trust protector," who can fire the trustee and hire a new trustee.

3. The APT is a "spendthrift trust," meaning it cannot be used to satisfy claims of future creditors.

4. The APT is irrevocable; meaning you generally cannot revoke it or change it. It may allow you to change the beneficiary of the trust, however.

5. The APT is not governed by the law of your state, but is governed by laws that make it less vulnerable to estate claims or to children's problems.

Whether your spouse creates this trust with assets exempt from Medicaid, or your children or other family members create it with assets acquired by gifts from you, the APT must be a "self-settled spendthrift trust." In other words, the creator of the trust must be able to protect the assets from his or her own creditors. Is the APT merely a modification of our regular living trust? Can it be drafted with ourselves or other family members as trustee?

We have one big stumbling block in merely altering a typical revocable living trust. Remember back in Chapter 10 we discussed the ancient English law called the Statute of Elizabeth? This law, carried forward into the United States, prevents a person from creating a trust that will allow him access to his assets and still protect it from creditors. Thus, no matter how we tinker with the living trust, so long as it is a trust based in a jurisdiction subject to the Statute of Elizabeth, it will be vulnerable to creditors, including Medicaid claims.

The key difference that makes an APT work is number 5 from the list above. The APT must choose as its governing law either the law of a country other than the U.S. or from one of the states that permit the overriding of the Statute of Elizabeth. If a foreign country is chosen, its law must also have overruled the Statute of Elizabeth.

There are a dozen or so countries that have their legal systems rooted in British law, yet have specifically overturned the Statute of Elizabeth. Some of the most noteworthy of these countries are the Bahamas, the Cook Islands, The Isle of Man, Nevis, and Belize. In addition, some states now allow some limited form of asset protection, such as Delaware and Alaska. For an APT to be an APT, it must be established in a jurisdiction such as one of these. Trusts created in these foreign countries have been used for decades by the wealthy to protect themselves from lawsuits. The same principles that make the APT attractive for the wealthy may make them cost-effective tools for Medicaid planning.

Unlike the foreign countries, Delaware and Alaska are new to this game. While you may feel comforted that your nest egg is not leaving the U.S., these trusts are yet to be tested as an asset protection plan.

The trustee of the APT will then be a trust company located in one of these nations or states. If you choose a foreign county, what other things do you look for that would make it a good choice for the "home" of your APT?

1. The foreign jurisdiction will generally not recognize a judgment or creditor claim obtained from a "foreign" (i.e., United States) court. This forces the creditor to re-litigate his or her claim in the court system where the trust is located. Thus, even if the state obtains a judg-

ment in a local court to satisfy a Medicaid claim, the judgment is worthless against the APT.

2. The foreign jurisdiction normally requires a plaintiff to use only attorneys licensed there, increasing the costs of litigating claims. So, if you die in the state of Missouri, and Missouri wants to impose a Medicaid claim against your APT, it will have to hire local lawyers in the country where your APT trustee is located.

3. The foreign jurisdiction typically prohibits contingent fee agreements, requiring the plaintiff to finance the litigation. In the United States, many lawsuits are brought by attorneys who will receive 33% to 40% of the amount recovered. The person bringing the suit does not need to lay out a large amount of money to file a lawsuit. This may not be permitted in the APT country.

4. The countries where APTs are located are as stable as the United States. They are democracies. The population generally enjoys a standard of living similar to ours. The local currency is normally pegged to the U.S. dollar. And most often, you can continue to hold your investments in U.S. dollars anyway.

5. These legal systems follow British common law. Trust law concepts are familiar and understandable.

6. These countries do not impose any taxes on the APT. From a U.S. tax standpoint, the APT is tax neutral. It does not save on income taxes. There are reporting requirements to the IRS when you create and maintain an APT. It does not increase your taxes either.

7. There are no currency restrictions on funds flowing into and out of the APT. The trustee can receive money into your trust and distribute it back to you or to whom you direct.

8. The laws in the country prohibit the APT trustee from revealing any information about the trust unless you approve.

9. Professional and competent trust companies are readily available, with costs similar to that of U.S. based banks and trust companies.

10. In the event of duress, as defined in the trust to include potential creditor action, the trustee may be mandated to: (a) discharge or ignore the trust protector, lessening any chance that a U.S. court can compel the trust protector to direct the trustee to take any acts that might expose the trust assets; (b) extend the term of the trust, to further frustrate creditors; or (c) transfer the trust to a second jurisdiction, so that even a persistent creditor must continue to "chase" the trust assets.

What are the biggest problems in creating and maintaining a foreign APT? Many persons fear dealing with a trustee in a foreign country. Some are afraid that the trustee will simply make off with their assets. Others have a "buy American" bent that makes them reluctant to entrust their affairs to a foreign trust company. Some are worried that they are somehow defrauding or cheating the government, and that the APT is a shady or dishonorable tool. With the advent of greater monitoring of international monetary systems due to terrorism concerns, the costs to do business in these foreign nations have risen dramatically in the last few years. This factor alone makes a foreign-based APT suitable only for situations where larger sums are to be protected: either more substantial gifts to children, or a higher spousal allowance permitted by a court.

Despite these issues, the countries that attract APTs have deliberately arranged their laws to seek this kind of business. Banking is usually one of the largest segments of the local economy. Thus, a country such as the Isle of Man or the Bahamas has a vested interest in maintaining standing as a safe, reputable place to do business. Trustees are licensed and regulated. Is it likely that the trustee is a crook? Probably as likely as in the U.S.

The notion of doing business only with American-based companies fades with the globalization of the banking industry. You may be surprised to find out who owns your local bank. For example, Harris Bank, a large Chicago based bank, is owned by the Bank of Montreal in Canada. The

LaSalle Banks are owned by Dutch interests. Many other "local" banks and trust companies are really parts of global business entities.

If you want to stay stateside, you can consider a trust based in Alaska or Delaware. Again, these are untested, and may in fact, be more expensive to maintain over time than most offshore financial centers, where the costs are generally lower.

What about the concept of frustrating the state's claim? Are you somehow committing fraud if you create an APT that protects inheritances from Medicaid estate claims?

The use of an APT is not a fraud upon the state. Review again the two ways in which an APT may be used.

Your spouse may use it to protect her spousal exempt assets. Remember that the regulations governing the Medicaid program permit a community spouse to transfer her assets after Medicaid eligibility is established. Whether that transfer is outright to children or other family or to an APT makes no difference. Neither is a fraud upon the state.

The other use of an APT occurs when it is created by family or children after the transfer of assets. The transfer period that affects Medicaid eligibility is over. The assets now legally belong to your children or other family members. They could not be subject to a Medicaid estate claim anyway. The APT is used to protect them from problems your children may encounter, not directly from the Medicaid claim.

So how is the typical APT integrated into a Medicaid plan? Let's look at a simple example.

EXAMPLE:

Abs Costello and his wife, Lu, earn $1,100 per month in social security. Frugal, they amassed $400,000 in assets, consisting mostly of bank accounts. They have two children, Stan and Ollie. Lu suffers a series of strokes that render her a nursing home resident. Ab petitions the court to allow additional assets to be retained by him in excess of his state's allowance of $101,640. The court order grants him the right to retain a total of $350,000 due to his limited income. He spends the remaining $50,000 on private pay care and applies for Medicaid. The application is approved, as the state Medicaid agency must honor the court order.

Ab then creates an APT in the Bahamas. He transfers his cash to the trust. The trustee, First APT Trust Company, will manage the assets for his benefit and will not change the investments unless Ab directs. Ab asks his accountant, Charlie Chapline, to act as trust protector for his APT. Accountant Chapline can fire First APT Trust for any reason or no reason at all, and hire a new trustee. This gives Ab comfort in knowing he, through his accountant, has some ultimate control over the trustee. The beneficiaries of the trust after Ab dies are Stan and Ollie. Ab dies four years later. The state sends out notice that it is seeking $105,000 in reimbursement for services it has provided for Lu. The state also wants to know why Lu is not a beneficiary of Ab's estate. The APT will help protect the assets for Stan and Ollie against these inquiries.

Did the APT cost Ab some money to create? Yes. Did Ab have to pay First APT Trust a yearly fee to manage the trust? Yes. The key question is how do these costs and fees stack up against the $105,000 claim? The costs and fees pale in comparison. The APT may be a cost effective component of Ab's Medicaid plan.

Our next chapter will look more at integrating APTs into some typical Medicaid plans. In fact, our next chapter is where we will look at not only plans in the Medicaid context, but also basic plans where Medicaid is not a concern. We will look at several examples that will "put it all together." Taking the total of the information in this book dealing with our three big issues—protecting assets upon incompetency, protecting assets upon death, and protecting assets from the nursing home—we will show how comprehensive plans can be developed to deal with these concerns.

16

Putting it All Together

Through the pages of fifteen prior chapters, we have learned much about the tools and techniques of asset protection planning for seniors. We looked at how incompetency can affect you and your spouse's ability to use and enjoy the assets for which you worked a lifetime. We saw some right ways to prepare an estate plan: ways that ensure your family will receive inheritances, protecting your estate from various perils. We also sampled the intricacies of the Medicaid system. We looked at how playing within these rules can help preserve your estate if you or your spouse need long-term care.

We journeyed through the art and science of asset protection planning. We did so cautioning you about taking a "one size fits all" approach, trying to fashion a given planning technique to your situation. Again, this is not a "how-to" book, nor is it a place to find forms or documents that will take care of your every need. Asset protection planning is individualized and complex. Trying to craft plans for every reader is at best irresponsible and at worst dangerous!

What we hope is that you understand the right questions to ask yourself. We also hope you understand some of the means by which plans can be made. You should walk away from this text at least knowing the three basic issues to cover in your legal affairs. You may also believe that you have a good grasp of such things as trusts, powers of attorney, and perhaps, even an asset protection trust. From these basics you, together with your attorney, accountant, and financial planner or other professional, can work as a team to formulate an effective asset protection plan of your own.

Our last chapter is about three families, albeit fictional ones, that looked at their situations and took steps to plan. These three final examples show how all the ideas and concepts we discussed can be woven together into a comprehensive approach to asset protection planning.

ASSET PROTECTION PLAN
EXAMPLE 1

Our first family, the Johns, is typical of many families across America. Dwight John and his wife, Mamie, raised three boys into manhood: Lyndon, Richard and Gerald. Lyndon is age 45, Richard is 41 and Gerald, the baby, is now age 35. Dwight is retired from his lifelong work and is enjoying retirement at age 72. Mamie, his wife of 50 years, is one year his junior. Both Dwight and Mamie have some of the usual minor maladies of aging but are basically in sound health.

Dwight and Mamie own their own home, and have paid off their mortgage prior to retirement. They have accumulated some investments through the years, as well as some small retirement accounts. They wish they could have done more saving for retirement, but raising three children and putting them through college took its toll. Nevertheless, they are quite content living on their retirement incomes of pensions and social security, dipping only now and then into their retirement nest egg for major needs or special occasions.

The John's financial picture looks like this:

Assets:

House, titled in joint tenancy between Dwight & Mamie	$ 150,000.
Savings account, also jointly owned	40,000.
Several mutual funds, also jointly owned	55,000.
Dwight's IRA, which lists Mamie as death beneficiary	60,000.
Mamie's IRA, which has no beneficiary listed	50,000.
Older automobile, jointly owned	3,500.
Checking account, 3-way joint tenancy with Richard	2,000.
Total assets:	$ 360,500.

Monthly Income:

Dwight's social security	$ 1,100.
Mamie's social security	560.
Dwight's pension	350.
Mamie's pension	100.
Approximate income from investments	500.
Total monthly income:	$ 2,610.

The Johns have old wills, made in 1968, which name guardians for their children. They also name Dwight's deceased sister as backup executor to each other. They have no other formal estate planning documents. They do not expect to receive any inheritances from any other family members at this time. Mamie's mother is still alive, at age 92, but she is in a nursing home. Medicaid is now paying for her care, as she used up her funds paying privately. The rapid depletion of her assets amazed the Johns.

Son Lyndon is married, with two children of his own. His marriage seems stable, and Dwight and Mamie are quite fond of Lyndon's wife and his children. Lyndon is a busy financial analyst for a local newspaper.

Richard is married also, for a second time, and his life is improving. Several years ago, Richard made a bad decision. He committed a "white collar" crime, for which he served 11 months in prison. Since then Richard has reformed and is doing quite well rebuilding his life. He has no children, but his second wife also has a good relationship with Dwight and Mamie. Richard is now employed by a city as a supervisor with the park district. He lives in a different state than his parents.

Gerald is the apple of his parents' eyes. He is a good-hearted soul, but alas, trouble seems to find him no matter where he goes. His shrew-like wife constantly battles with Gerald and Mamie. He has three children, and a myriad of financial problems that resulted in a bankruptcy two years ago. Dwight and Mamie hope that Gerald will begin to restore his financial life. They dislike his wife, but believe that marriage is forever, and reluctantly accept that she is a part of their family. Gerald is a paramedic with the city fire department.

The Johns' best friend, Roosevelt Truman, dies. Mrs. Truman has to go to court to probate Roosevelt's estate. Her stories about the court system spur the Johns into action. They decide to see their lawyer to update their estate plans. With the help of their attorney, the Johns identify several concerns that need to be addressed in their new estate plans:

- They wish to avoid probate, whether it would be triggered by the first spouse to die or the second.

- They want some ability for either spouse to access the family assets.

- While both are fairly healthy, if either needs a nursing home, they want to prevent the estate depletion that Mamie's mother experienced.

- They want some way to protect a child, particularly Richard or Gerald, from a divorcing spouse, creditor or other problem wasting an inheritance meant for them.

- They understand that estate taxation is not a concern for them.

- They learn that they should have someone designated to make healthcare decisions for them if they are unable.

Based on these things, their lawyer prepares for them a new estate plan.

The Johns execute a joint revocable living trust. They are co-trustees and co-beneficiaries of the trust for life. Son Lyndon is named as successor trustee, and First National Bank as second successor trustee. The Johns do not believe that either Richard or Gerald would be an appropriate successor trustees. After both spouses die, the trust divides equally among all three boys. However, the trust continues unless a beneficiary voluntarily requests his share. The trust also contains a spendthrift clause. The Johns put these provisions in the trust in the event that Richard or Gerald encounters stormy seas. The trust also allows an agent under a power of attorney to withdraw funds from the trust.

Accompanying the trust are two "pour over" wills. The Johns' lawyer explains that once the revocable trust is "funded"—that is, the assets are placed within it—the wills would generally distribute only personal effects.

The John's each create a durable power of attorney for property. These powers of attorney name each other as agent and son Lyndon as successor agent. The powers of attorney permit an agent to withdraw funds from the

Johns' trust and to deal with assets in such a way as to protect them in the event a nursing home is needed.

Finally, they have their attorney prepare durable powers of attorney for healthcare for both of them. Again, they name each other as agent and Lyndon as successor agent.

With this estate plan in place, the Johns have met all the concerns they presented to their lawyer. They have dealt with the three big asset protection concerns we studied in this book: problems relating to incompetency; disposition of assets upon death, without probate and taking into account potential difficulties that may beset a beneficiary; and a plan to deal with a nursing home situation, if and only if it arises, without drastically altering their assets or current lifestyle.

ASSET PROTECTION PLAN
EXAMPLE 2

Our second couple presents a different picture from the Johns. Ben is age 75, and a widower. He never had any children, but has several nieces and nephews of whom he is fond. All of the nieces and nephews are adults and quite stable. Ben lives with Gerry, a spry widow of 76. Gerry has two daughters from her previous marriage. Both daughters also lead peaceful lives.

Ben owns a house where he and Gerry live together. They are not married. They share living expenses from their incomes. They have old, outdated wills from when they were married to their now deceased spouses.

Ben and Gerry want to "take care of each other"; however, when both are gone, Ben wants his estate to go to his nephews, nieces and some charities. Gerry wants her meager estate to go to her two daughters. If a daughter should predecease Gerry, that daughter's share should be split among that daughter's children.

Ben's financial picture looks like this:

Assets:

House, titled in Ben's name alone, with no mortgage	$180,000.
Various bank accounts, titled jointly with Gerry	55,000.
Mutual funds and other securities, in Ben's name alone	490,000.
Total assets:	$ 725,000.

Gerry's financial picture looks like this:

Assets:

Bank accounts, titled jointly with her two daughters	$ 9,000.
IRA account, with no beneficiary	5,500.
Older automobile, titled in Gerry's name	1,000.
US savings bonds	4,500.
Total assets:	$ 20,000.

Their monthly incomes are quite sufficient for them to live on:

Monthly Income:

Ben's pension	$ 2,200.
Ben's social security	1,100.
Ben's income from investments	3,000.
—approximate	
Gerry's pension	1,000.
Gerry also receives a survivor	1,400.
pension from her late	
husband's company	
Gerry's income from investments	minimal

Total monthly incomes:

Ben	$ 6,300
Gerry	$ 2,400

Ben and Gerry each visit separate local attorneys. Their attorneys prepare estate plans for each.

Gerry's estate plan is rather basic. She signs a simple will that leaves her assets outright equally to her two daughters upon death. If a daughter pre-deceases her, the one-half share will go to that daughter's children. Gerry makes no provision for Ben, as he is well enough off to live on his own if she should die first. Gerry need not worry about probate of her estate, because her state allows settling an estate under $100,000 with a small estates affidavit. In addition, the joint tenancies on some of her assets would avoid probate anyway. She designates her two daughters as death beneficiaries of her IRA account.

Gerry also signs durable powers of attorney for property and healthcare. She names her daughters as agent and successor agent for property. She decides to name Ben as first agent for healthcare and her daughters as backups.

Gerry does not put any planning in her documents for a nursing home. Her assets are too meager to consider protection, as $20,000 may not even allow her admission into a quality nursing home as it is.

Ben's attorney recommends a declaration of trust for him, with a pour over will as an ancillary document. Ben is trustee of the trust, with First State Bank and Trust as successor trustee. Upon his death, Ben's trust leaves the house outright to Gerry. He also leaves some of the joint bank accounts titled jointly with Gerry, so she would receive these on his death. The rest of his assets—the other bank accounts and the mutual funds and securities—would remain in trust for Gerry's lifetime. The trustee will pay the income of the trust to Gerry, and will also pay out principal to her, but only as necessary to supplement her needs. Gerry's interest in the trust would immediately end if she needed care in a nursing home. As Ben is not married to Gerry, he has no legal obligation to use his assets for her nursing home care.

Ben's trust will terminate on one of three events: (1) if he dies first, and then Gerry dies, the trust ends; (2) if Gerry dies first, then Ben's trust will end upon his death; or (3) if Ben dies first, but Gerry enters a nursing home, the trust will terminate. Upon the termination of the trust, Ben's nephews, nieces, and favorite charities are the beneficiaries.

Ben also signs two durable powers of attorney: one for property and one for healthcare. He names Gerry as agent under both. He does not choose to name a successor. He also signs a living will in case he is terminally ill and Gerry can no longer be his healthcare agent due to her prior death or incompetency.

Ben also does not put any asset protection planning into his documents for a nursing home situation. His monthly income will more than likely cover any nursing home he might need. Even if his income were to fall short, the depletion of his assets would be so slow that he would likely pass away before his estate was substantially diminished.

Both estate plans, while different, deal with all the big issues. Neither estate should be probated; both name beneficiaries according to what Ben and Gerry want. Both Ben and Gerry have provided for the problems incompetency might cause, through uses of powers of attorney and even a living will. Medicaid will provide for Gerry without any additional planning if she needs nursing home care. Ben's income and assets are sufficient to care for him. Finally, Ben's trust has charities as some of the ultimate beneficiaries. Ben will owe no estate tax because his taxable estate is less than the current federal estate tax exemption.

ASSET PROTECTION PLAN
EXAMPLE 3

Our final couple is again a typical American family. Amadeus Smith and his lovely wife of 50 years, Ludwiga, have two children, Frederic and Johann. Amadeus is 74 years old, and Ludwiga is 72. Frederic, age 44, is married with two fine children of his own. He earns a good living as a middle manager for a local business. Johann is a single 42 year old who is a hard-driving and successful attorney.

Amadeus noticed that he was having some difficulties with his memory. He was getting lost trying to drive the car. He was forgetting people's names. He sometimes would wake in the middle of the night and be confused as to time of day. He went to his physician, Dr. Bach. Dr. Bach ran a battery of tests and diagnosed Amadeus with probable Alzheimer's disease. Physically, Amadeus is quite healthy.

Ludwiga is also physically healthy, but the prospect of caring for Amadeus at home already overwhelms her. She and the children both realize that Amadeus requires 24-hour supervision. They hope that he would not need to be in a nursing facility, but they are unsure how they would pay for care at home. Financially, the Smiths are solidly middle class.

The Smith's financial picture looks like this:

Assets:

Bank accounts, certificates of	$ 40,000.
deposit, all titled jointly	
between the Smiths	
Annuity owned by Ludwiga	
(purchased prior to 2/06)	$ 125,000.
Amadeus' IRA,	55,000.
listing Ludwiga as beneficiary	
Ludwiga's IRA,	3,500.
listing Amadeus as beneficiary	
Various stocks and bonds,	45,000.
titled jointly	
Total assets:	$ 268,500.

Monthly Income:

Amadeus' social security	$ 1,000.
Amadeus' musician's union pension	450.
Ludwiga's social security	900.
Investment income	1,115.
Total monthly income:	$ 3,465.

About three years ago, the Smiths had simple wills and durable powers of attorney for property and healthcare prepared. The property powers name each other as agent. These powers also allow the agent to transfer property to the spouse, e.g. Ludwiga, acting as Amadeus' agent, can transfer any of his property to herself.

Ludwiga and her sons look at various nursing homes. Baroque Acres is chosen as a good facility for Amadeus. Baroque Acres accepts Medicaid.

The facility would like Amadeus to be able to pay for at least one year privately. They would like financial statements indicating that before they will admit him.

The Smiths return to their attorney, Mr. Brahms, for advice. Their attorney drafts the following plan.

First, they will use Amadeus' IRA to pay for private pay nursing care. The $55,000 will cover at least a year in Baroque Acres. Funds taken out of the IRA are subject to income tax. However, the cost of care that the Smith's pay to Baroque Acres will be tax deductible. Thus, the tax deduction will offset any federal income tax the Amadeus' might pay on the IRA withdrawals.

Ludwiga also decides to cash in her IRA. Again, this is taxable, but it is a small sum.

Ludwiga purchases pre-paid funerals involving cremation for herself and Amadeus. Total cost: $8,000. She makes sure that the funeral plans she makes will qualify under her state's Medicaid rules. These are paid for from the money from the two IRA accounts.

Attorney Brahms advises her son, Johann, to prepare an estate plan. As a single adult, his estate would pass to his mother and father if he met with a sudden demise.

Ludwiga executes a new will disinheriting Amadeus, and new powers of attorney that name her sons, and not her husband as agents.

Ludwiga also creates an asset protection trust, with Seaside Bank and Trust in Alaska as trustee. Ludwiga is the beneficiary of this trust for her life, with her two boys as death beneficiaries. Into this trust, Ludwiga places the securities, the annuity, and most of the remaining cash she has on hand. The trustee annuitizes the annuity on Ludwiga's life. Because it was purchased prior to the 2006 change in the rules, the annuity qualifies as an exempt asset under local Medicaid rules.

Amadeus enters Baroque Acres. In a year Ludwiga has spent about $50,000 on private pay care. Her asset picture now looks like this:

Asset Protection Trust:

Cash and securities on hand	$ 80,000.
Annuity	125,000.

Other Assets

Prepaid funerals	8,000.
Cash on hand in checking account	5,000.

Ludwiga applies for Medicaid to pay Amadeus' cost of care. Her application is approved. The state views the annuity and the funeral plans as exempt assets. The cash and securities, whether held within the trust or in her checking account are also exempt, as they are within her spousal allowance amount in her state.

Ludwiga keeps all her social security and all the income from the trust. She receives some of Amadeus' income to supplement her income and to bring her up to the monthly income allowed by her state's Medicaid rules.

Amadeus receives Medicaid assistance for three years. Suddenly, Ludwiga has a heart attack and dies. The state looks for $70,000 from Ludwiga's estate to compensate it for supporting Amadeus in the nursing home. It also wants Ludwiga's estate to include Amadeus as a beneficiary, as he is still going strong in the nursing home. The asset protection trust managed by Seaside Bank and Trust is protected from these claims and demands.

The Smith plan created additional exempt assets by purchasing funeral plans and the annuitizing of a pre-existing annuity. The Smith plan also protected the family inheritance for Johann and Frederic. The Smith family is an example of a Medicaid situation where the need for planning was imminent. It is also an example of how cost effective these plans can be. While the asset protection trust took some funds to create and administer, it saved the family a great deal in estate claims and forced heirship problems. As an added bonus, the asset protection trust will also afford the most comprehensive asset protection for Johann and Frederic, should they decide to leave their inheritances in trust.

These three examples are greatly oversimplified. You may read these and think that your situation is similar, but in reality you probably differ on several points. This is precisely why asset protection planning is so individualized. In every way we are different. Thus, in every way, we need a plan tailored to our own particular situation.

Our hope is that you now know the right questions, if not all the right answers. You should also be familiar with terms and tools used in the planning process. The next steps are yours. Take what you have learned to your own attorney, accountant, financial planner, or other advisers. All the information in the world will not help if you fail to use it: good luck!

Glossary

Term	Definition
Accounting	A listing of all assets of an estate, showing income and expenditures, prepared by a guardian, executor or administrator.
Administrative Law Judge	The person whom presides over disputes involving government agencies.
Administrator	The person or corporation appointed by the court in an intestate estate to gather the assets of the estate, administer the estate, and arrange for distribution of the assets according to statute.
Advance Medical Directives	An individual's written instructions to the medical community, which recites the individual's wishes regarding life-sustaining treatment.
Agent	A person appointed by another to act in the place of, and for the benefit of, that individual.
Ancillary Probate	Additional probate proceeding in a state where the decedent had real estate but did not reside.
Annuity	Fixed, periodic payments over a person's lifetime or over a certain number of years.
Bequest	A gift of personal property by will.
Claims	In a probate proceeding, a demand for money due a creditor of the estate.
Claims Period	In a probate proceeding, the time period in which creditors can demand payment from the estate.
Codicil	An amendment to a will which explains, modifies, adds to, subtracts from, alters or revokes certain provisions of the will.

Community Spouse	Medicaid term: spouse of a nursing home resident who does not reside in the nursing home.
Community Spouse Resource Allowance	Medicaid term: the maximum amount of assets a community spouse is allowed to keep.
Conservatorship	The office of an individual legally appointed by the court to manage the affairs of an incompetent individual—synonymous with guardian of the estate.
Contingent	Beneficiaries who are next in line should the primary beneficiaries die before collecting their share.
The Court	A term often used to refer to the judge presiding over a matter.
Decedent	Refers to a deceased person.
Disabled person/ward	An individual who has been declared unfit by the court to handle his own affairs.
Disclaimer	The written refusal of the right to any interest in an estate.
Estate	Refers to all that an individual owns.
Estate Beneficiary	The recipient of the assets of an estate according to the terms of a will.
Executor	The person or corporation named in a will and appointed by the Court, who will gather the assets of the estate, pay claims, administer the estate and arrange for distribution of the assets according to the terms of the will.
Exempt Assets	Medicaid term: those assets which are not considered available to pay for cost of nursing home care, and thus may be kept by the individual or his spouse.
Fair Market Value (FMV)	The price at which property can be sold in a market of willing buyers and sellers in the ordinary course of business.
Guardian *ad litem*	Representative, often an attorney, appointed by the court to look after the interests of an alleged disabled person or minor in connection with a court controversy such as a guardianship.

Guardian of the Estate	In a guardianship proceeding, the authority of a legally appointed individual to manage the finances and property of a disabled person—synonymous with conservator.
Guardian of the Person	In a guardianship proceeding, the authority of a legally appointed individual to manage the healthcare decisions of a disabled person.
Healthcare Proxy	Written document whereby an individual appoints an agent to make healthcare decisions for him should he become incapacitated.
Heir	An individual who, by statute, is entitled to receive the assets of the estate of a deceased ancestor or relative by right of his kinship to the ancestor or relative.
Incompetency/incapacity	The inability or lack of fitness to manage one's affairs.
Independent administration	Administration of a probate estate by its representative without court supervision.
Inheritance	Assets to be distributed to an heir.
Initial Determination	Medicaid term: the decision made by the Department of Public Aid after review of the application and supporting documents.
***In terrorem* clause**	Provision in a will or trust designed to threaten a beneficiary with forfeiture of his interest if the beneficiary disputes the validity or disposition of the will or trust.
Intestate estate	Estate of an individual who died without leaving a will.
Inventory	List of a decedent's assets; also refers to the assets of a disabled individual in a guardianship proceeding.
IRA	Individual Retirement Account: a tax deferred account, used as a retirement planning tool, where the account funds are generally unavailable, without a tax penalty, until age 59-1/2.
Irrevocable trust	A trust which can only be terminated under its own terms; its creator retains no right to terminate the trust.
Joint tenancy	A form of ownership in which two or more people share title to an asset equally at the same time.

Lack of capacity	Lacking the mental ability to understand the effect of one's actions.
Legatee	The recipient of personal property under a will.
Lien	A claim upon the property of another as security for a debt; e.g., a mortgage is a type of lien.
Life-sustaining Medical Treatment	The use of artificial or mechanical means to sustain life, whose primary use is to prolong life when death is imminent.
Limited Power of Appointment	The right retained by the maker of a deed, or other document disposing of property, to change the person or persons who may receive the property upon the occurrence of a certain event as specified in the deed or document.
Living Trust	A trust which exists during the life of the creator.
Living Will	A directive to a physician where one refuses life-sustaining care in the event of a hopeless illness.
Long-term Care Insurance	Insurance for the purpose of offsetting costs in the event of a prolonged nursing home stay.
Marital Trust	A trust created for the benefit of a surviving spouse.
Medicaid	A joint federal-state program that provides for payment of nursing home costs under certain circumstances.
Medicare	A federal health insurance program covering groups such as senior citizens.
Non-exempt Assets	Medicaid term: those assets which must be spent on private pay nursing home care.
Non-probate Estate	All assets of a decedent that pass to designated beneficiaries without the need for probate court proceedings.
Payable on death	Designation whereby an asset has a beneficiary stated upon the death of the owner.
Per stirpes	Refers to descendants of a deceased ancestor standing in the ancestor's place to inherit property to which the deceased ancestor had a right.
Plenary Guardian	The representative appointed by the court to act on behalf of a disabled person or minor who has the fullest powers allowed by law to so act.

Post-eligibility Transfer	Medicaid term: refers to transfers of assets by the community spouse after the nursing home spouse gains eligibility for Medicaid assistance.
Power of Attorney for Health-care	A written document in which one individual (the principal) names another individual (the agent) to act in his place if he should be unable to communicate his health-care wishes to the medical community; a "durable" power remains in effect even if the principal is found disabled in a guardianship proceeding.
Power of Attorney for Property	A written document in which one individual (the principal) names another individual (the agent) to act in his place if he should be unable to manage his financial affairs; a "durable" power remains in effect even if the principal is found disabled in a guardianship proceeding.
Pre-marital Agreement	An agreement between an engaged couple that attempts to resolve property division issues in the event of a future divorce or death.
Probate	A court proceeding to determine if a will is valid, or if there is no will, who is entitled to a decedent's assets.
Renounce/property renunciation	The written act of a surviving spouse refusing the property to be received under a will, if any, and instead taking the share allowed by statute.
Residue	The portion of a probate estate that remains after debts and bequests have been paid.
Revocable Trust	A trust, which can be altered, changed, amended or terminated by its creator.
Self-canceling Installment Note	Evidence of a loan to be repaid in specified amounts over a certain time period where, upon the occurrence of an event, i.e. death of the lender, the loan will be forgiven.
Self-declaration of Trust	A written document created by an individual in which title is held initially by the creator as trustee to be held for the benefit of the creator.
Settlor/Grantor	Creator of a trust.

Small Estates Affidavit	Document used to pass a decedent's assets to heirs and legatees when an estate has too few assets to probate.
Spendthrift Clause	Language in a trust that prohibits creditors from gaining access to a beneficiary's share.
Springing Power	Authority granted upon the occurrence of a specific event.
Statute of Elizabeth	English law, adopted in the United States and in most of the former English colonies, which prohibits a person from creating a trust with his own assets that is sheltered from his own creditors.
Step-up in Basis	An increase in the income tax basis of property; results when heirs receive appreciated property from a decedent.
Supervised Administration	Administration of a probate estate by its representative where each action of the representative must be overseen and approved by a court.
Supplemental Needs Trust	A trust that provides for needs of a beneficiary other than those things for which a governmental program pays.
Surety Bond	An agreement where a surety, usually an insurance company, for a fee, guarantees that a guardian or executor will handle the duties of his office in good faith.
Temporary Guardian	An interim representative appointed by the court to act on behalf of an individual during the time prior to the appointment of a full, plenary guardian.
Testamentary	An event that occurs after death.
Testamentary Trust	A trust created under the terms of a will which only comes into existence when a will is admitted to probate.
Testate Estate	Estate of an individual who died leaving a will.
Trust Beneficiary	The recipient of the assets of the trust in accordance with the instructions of the grantor.
Trust protector	An individual who has certain powers to control or direct the trustee of a trust; typically used with a foreign trust.

Trustee	The individual or corporation that holds legal title to all assets contained in a trust.
Undue influence	To coerce or pressure another person so that his free will is compromised.
Will	A written document, executed according to statute, by which an individual makes provision for the disposition of his property after his death.

978-0-595-45777-9
0-595-45777-0